HÜMÜH Transcendental Buddhist

Maticintin

Wisdom Master

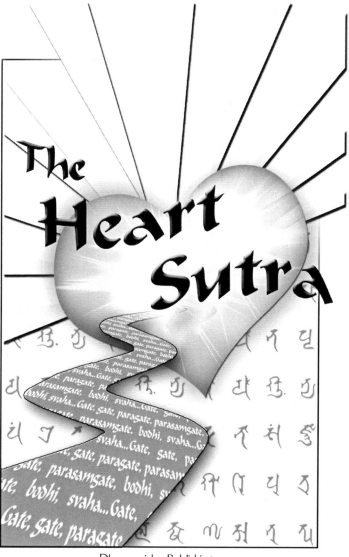

Dharmavidya Publishing

2008

The Heart Sutra

International Copyright © 2008 Maticintin
Printed in the United States of America
Dharmavidya Publishing

ISBN: 978-0-932927-26-2

Decipher and Commentary by Wisdom Master Maticintin
Scribe: Mary Daniels
Text Design: Jennifer Bratton
Cover Design: Monika Mueller

DHARMAVIDYA PUBLISHING

P.O. Box 2700, Oroville, WA 98844 USA
or P.O. Box 701, Osoyoos, B.C. V0H 1V0 Canada
Phone/fax (250) 446-2022 / Phone Orders (800) 336-6015
E-mail: DharmavidyaPublishing@HUMUH.org

Table of Contents

Wisdom Master Maticintin

Wisdom Master Maticintin is a vessel of the Mind Treasure Teachings, gifted her by the Transhistorical Consciousness, meaning she attained enlightenment in another lifetime. The Wisdom Master also has a Doctorate in Logic and Buddhism and is the Founder and Spiritual Leader of HÜMÜH: Transcendental Buddhism, Path to Enlightenment. Currently in residence at the HÜMÜH Monastery in British Columbia, Wisdom Master Maticintin teaches there at Skycliffe Retreat Centre's Transcendental Awareness Institute. She also travels and teaches in the United States, Canada, and, occasionally, abroad.

Wisdom Master Maticintin is a noted author with many books to her credit, among them *Shaman of Tibet*, the story of Milarepa, and *The Golden Spiral: Handbook for Enlightenment*. She has been a student of Buddhism for more than 30 years, holds a Doctorate in Divinity, and is also the Shaman known as Winged Wolf.

While keeping up with a year-round Teaching schedule, the Wisdom Master maintains periods of solitude in between working with her students and takes time to be in companion energy with a herd of 50 wild deer, a horse named Spirit, a donkey called Pepe, and a romping red-haired Pomeranian named Dorji.

She brought forth HÜMÜH in 1992 as an expression of primordial wisdom that directly addresses the Western body/mind connection. One of the manifestations of her dedication as a Teacher is the Home-Study program she has developed that enables students to work with her at a distance, as well as through on-site retreats and classes. The spiritual path of HÜMÜH began in the United States and has rapidly expanded into Canada, while developing membership in a variety of other countries.

Introduction

When I was five, I was visited at my family home by an Asian monk, who gave me two gifts: One was a little brown book about the Tibetan adept Milarepa, and the other a message he had inscribed inside the front cover of the book – *Mahaprajnaparamita*, which I was later to find out was an epithet for The Heart Sutra.

For many years after that, I dreamed about the monk. Sometimes, those dreams occurred when I was asleep, and sometimes when I was awake, playing in the forest behind my family's house. Sometimes, he leaped from my memory and became flesh and blood again, which usually occurred when I pulled the small brown book from beneath my mattress, the hiding place of all my private treasures. In these times, he assisted me in solving difficult situations in my daily life.

Throughout my youth, over and over, I read the book about Milarepa he had given me. At some point, during those years, I drew an unsuspecting heart with radiance lines coming off of it around the inscription *Mahaprajnaparamita*. No one in my family knew what the inscription meant, and Buddhism was not a subject that was readily available in our home or community during that time, and so it was not until many years later that I actually learned what it meant.

All the same, my attraction to Buddhism was gleaned from those early experiences. Then, in the late 1960's, I affiliated myself with, first, the Nichiren sect of Buddhism and then with Zen. In 1970, I traveled to Japan and became a young monk studying in that country. During the time that I was there, over a year, I submerged myself in the haunting mantra – *Gate! Gate! Paragate...Parasamgate...Bodhi, Svaha!* – which has continued to live on the edge of my consciousness to this day.

If you are a spiritual student seeking enlightenment, the 'Decipher' that has unfolded from my own awakened consciousness, will guide the way for you. Read it over and over while making the *Mahaprajnaparamita* mantra a part of your life.

Maticintin

The Heart Sutra
Text

The Heart Sutra

गते

गते

परगते परसंगते

बोधि स्वहा
(Sanskrit)

Gate!
Gate!
Paragate...Parasamgate...
Bodhi, Svaha!
(Transliteration)

Gone!
Gone!
Gone to the beyond,
and beyond the beyond!
O prajna paramita
Rejoice!
(Translation)

Decipher
The Heart Sutra

The gradual way
does not lead to liberation.
Because it is gradual, it goes nowhere -
like a heart beating in the wind
contributes nothing to the air.
Why, then, do people seek the gradual way?
Because they like to pretend.

Whereas to Awaken,
one must enter the heart.
And while the gateway is simple to navigate,
the access into its chamber is illusive.

Here
in this glorious place known as Skycliffe,
we gather to put aside all things
for the sake of realizing
that without burdens and limitations,
items of personality,
we inherit ALL.

Personality,
having no real self-substance,
devises creations that are based on sensations,
perceived by miniscule viewpoints,
and tied together by likenesses that evaporate
like droplets of water in hot air.
If, however,
we realize this, we can instead,
use personality as a Divine Tool.

As a Divine Tool,
personality is freed within the Great Ocean.
Its talents then rise up from unfathomable depths ...
from within the sacred sea.
Then,
whenever rapture between Heart and Purpose connect,
the cause is complete, and
the Prajna clears.

As such, in samsara,
the Divine Tool whispers intuitively.
Whatever needs to be known is known,
including situational directions,
any knowledge of existence – both sentient and non-sentient –
as well as life and death.
It begins in this way ...

All phenomena are seen as indications
and assertions,
which means it is empty of entity.
Even though the heart pumps blood to sustain the body, and
the spirit prompts the mind,
no entity is present, only containers of energy.
Thus,
the Prajna is free of controls and, instead,
responds from clairvoyant choice.

Listen !
Intuition cannot exist without free-will.
In this way, the mind has not been transferred (to an entity),
and the objects of transference
have not arisen.
In a mirror, when the reflection of a face appears,
it appears without a face, the reflection being transferred
from face to object ... like dreams in sleep;
like waves, which are the nature of water;
rivers flowing in four directions
are the same in the ocean.

So ...
Mind and primordial wisdom are like moisture
and its water;
Is and is not demonstrate a mind
that is apprehending.

There is nothing to do, and no doer to do it.
By liberating
denial and assertions into the primordial,
happiness will be achieved.

All
deliberate concepts are fabrications.
If whatever arises, arises free
from conceptual reasoning,
it is Primordial Wisdom —
sudden purity Primordial Awareness.
The realization that results,
is that the phenomenon of the world and beings,
are the naturally pure Buddha-Field.

The Heart
beats purely in a Buddha-Field,
laced with dharma-thread.
Here, life is lived beyond the surface of the mirror
where ordinary life is usually lived.
This is an entrance into utter silence,
a realm where not a single thought is born.
When gazing outward from this agreeable place,
suddenly one forgets the gazing; all
objects disappear without a trace
and you can't even find your own body.
This is a time when heaven enters earth.
Then...

whatever arises, be it strong desire, aversions, or
even pleasure over riches, represents
only the manifestation of the creative energy
of intrinsic awareness.
This is very much unlike the undercurrent of thoughts,
deriving unnoticed from mind, which
accumulates endless future karma
in the prison samsara.

To Become
a Wisdom Master, one passes through the heart
and is gone,
gone,
gone to the beyond,
and beyond the beyond.

As the journey begins,
unforeseen forces tear at the fabric of one's life
and life force.
Moaning in fever, the Traveler shifts in spirit
in a way that causes synchronization
of multiple energies.
Thus, allowances for adjustments are made.

Gone ...
Upon first passing through the Heart,
one touches upon the place where prayers arrive.
It is here that one realizes self as compassion.
Charity arises here and one volunteers
to suffer to relieve suffering.

Gone ...
When sufferings flows through,
then the concession has been made,
and the second stage
has been opened to pass through.
This second Heart Chamber stage is all-knowing.
Heaven and earth inaudibly whisper
the archives of primordial knowledge to the Traveler
from which others can be enlightened.

Gone to the beyond ...
Beyond the bounds; clear of 'farther,'
cryptic silence pervades all space.
Movements are light-filled with grace.
Everywhere the attention goes
unrestricted energies glow.
Here, miraculous apparitions arise without effort,
and thus ignite unconstrained and unequivocal love.

Beyond the beyond ...
Wordless and unspeakable, incommunicable and
inconceivable; unimaginable and unbelievable
is the unutterable realm,
a place so 'real' that it is non-existent,
beyond memory and echo.
Rapture prolongs ecstasy.
Sustained rapture opens to para-nirvana, whereas
intermittent rapture returns to earth.

If you want to travel these realms,
listen to and contemplate the great mysterious mantra:
Gate, gate, paragate, parasamgate, bodhi, svaha!
which translates:
Gone, gone, gone to beyond, and beyond the beyond,
O prajna paramita
Rejoice!

Maticintin, Wisdom Master

The Heart Sutra
Commentary

The gradual way

does not lead to liberation.

Because it is gradual, it goes nowhere—

like a heart beating in the wind

contributes nothing to the air.

Why, then, do people seek the gradual way?

Because they like to pretend.

The last word of the stanza is *pretend, which* seems like an insult at first, but is not intended that way. It's intended to bring forth an image of the feeling that we want to be known as knowing something, and wanting to be *known as 'knowing' something, is pretense and not real. Often, people who are attracted to a gradual way* learn facts and figures that they can then espouse without assuming responsibility for what they espouse; pretenders. This means that they have acquired only superficial knowledge, rather than actual or divine knowledge.

The *gradual way* does not demand that we *live* what we espouse; it simply gives us an opportunity to intellectually accumulate knowledge in the same way that we accumulate goods. Such accumulation of knowledge leads us to attach feelings to the bits of information that we acquire. Even though we gain insights about these, such insights often remain disjointed, out of context. A heartbeat in a blowing wind causes no effect upon the wind. Likewise, the *gradual way* cannot produce enlightenment, because by its nature, such a person working on a gradual level always holds back, lacking wholeheartedness. The gradual way can, however, refine one's character to be a better person, but being a better person, in itself, or virture by itself, cannot cause us to spiritually awaken; goodness, of itself, does not take us into the heart of Buddhahood. Instead, such are preparatory stages of virtuous karma.

The *gradual way* of doing things is usually geared to limitations that please other people, so that we get pleasure in return from them, which is then our reward, rather than living as a bodhisattva, whereby one doesn't think of oneself while giving, but instead, simply gives because the giving is there to do; and that, in itself, is the reward. When the latter is the case, then there is *spiritual evolvement*.

The *gradual way* espouses a calculated-to-observe-its-gain step forward. One who espouses the *gradual way* is always looking at self and self's feelings. As it looks at self and self's feelings, it performs good deeds, but like a trained monkey, expecting a coin in a cup. Relationships, then, exist to benefit self, which is why such relationships fail. True companionship, on the other hand, concerns each person walking together with the other; each strengthening themselves through a mutual bond, and sharing from that.

So, the *gradual way* is not a way that leads to liberation.

Whereas to Awaken,

one must enter the heart.

And while the gateway is simple

to navigate, the access

into its chamber

is illusive.

Access into the chamber is illusive, because we have to get past the place of not wanting to accept responsibility for conditions in our lives. Instead, we must learn to accept the edict that all conditions are contained in one's mind as a result of one's mental concepts and notions concerning physical reality. This is the most difficult thing that we initiate—taking actual responsibility for everything that occurs in our life, even though we may feel somebody offended, or benefited us. All situations play out according to our mental states, and our mental states come about through thoughts and mental imagery that we carry within ourselves. So, this responsibility is still *ours,* no matter what anybody else does in a situation. Even if someone runs up behind us and strikes us with a club. Perhaps we weren't thinking to ourselves that somebody was going to run up and strike us with a club, but there was something in our mental makeup that attracted that type of thunderous response. This can be really difficult for us to accept, that all conditions are products of our mind. We have to truly witness things as they're happening, and to witness things as they're happening means that we've already established a degree of awareness of this nature. To have this degree of mindfulness means that we are experiencing Third Eye Vision, which has the power to correct poor health.

Financial worries can result if one hates to give. If we monitor ourselves and how our attitudes and opinions play out, we'll see why the *gradual way* is not the course that we want to take, because it is bound to attitudes and opinions, and therefore, it can't take us anywhere valuable; attitudes and opinions often produce spoiled fruit.

Being bound by attitudes and opinions is a pronouncement of our viewpoints. Whether or not these viewpoints were adopted from somebody else or not, we added our little tidbit to them, as well, so it is still *our* responsibility that we're carrying them. We cannot fault others for our viewpoints; our acceptance of the viewpoints we carry are our personal responsibilities. If we become aware of such an attitude in action, we can dissolve it through the removal of our attention from it.

One of the most troublesome parts of ourselves is *ego*....One's ego likes to think that somebody else did something *to* them. Likewise, if it was something good, the ego likes to think that it had *sole* responsibility for it. In fact, it does, because we are the creators, but at the same time, the creations of our lives (friendships, as well) work cooperatively with us. Our creations (situations) work cooperatively with us when our mental state is open to the harmony of cooperative creation.

The *gradual way*, being bound in attitudes and opinions, self-centeredness, says, *"I don't want to go too fast. I'm enjoying myself too much in what I'm doing. I'm going to play this out, and play that out. Then, when I am done with that, why then, I may want to really educate myself spiritually or awaken spiritually, but right now, I just want to do something else."* As we shift our attention to something else, one thing leads to another, and we become oblivious, lost. As we become lost in oblivion, problems arise that *appear* so paramount, so dominant in life, that we forget that we are their creator. So, people die from health problems, and they suffer from financial problems, and they suffer from separation from their attachments in life. The *gradual way* is a deadly way, and there is no arrival point or destination to it, and it is addictive, as well. It has this illusion attached to it that this is the way life is, that we are victims.

This prologue to the *Heart Sutra* gives us information that the *gradual way* isn't going to take us there. We make our lives what we want them to be through mental and physical adjustments. Such adjustments will come to pass as we begin to set things in motion towards what we want, rather than clinging to what we don't want. We have to set free what we don't want by no longer abiding with it in our lives. What do we want? That's what we keep our attention on. If we truly live for what we want to achieve in life, we'll find that we're developing spiritually, and if we're developing spiritually, then the *good of the whole* is what results.

Only the bold and adventuresome will attain the spiritualized consciousness.

We have to look *deeply* at what we do want, not superficially, because if we're living a spiritual life as a creator, we can have anything. Truly, the only course of action toward what we want in life has to tie in with spirituality; otherwise, it's just an object. Why would a creator lust after an object? The creator can *create* anything.

Learning to be the creator means that we have learned to live for the good of the whole; since we're a part of the whole, we are completely satisfied with our role in life, and it is ever-expanding and ever-awakening, and we want for nothing.

So the *Heart Sutra* sets up a periscope, so that we can see the life around us through true eyes, never forgetting that we are the creators. Our circumstances cannot change, or improve, or get worse, without our assistance, without our direction. Having a flash of understanding about something does us no good at all, unless we put intuition into practice in our lives. If we have a flash of intuition and then pull back,...we have yielded to a weakened position of the *gradual way*. It takes us nowhere—because we have pulled back, instead of using what we have learned.

We have to decide what we *really* want, not rely on excuses for or against what we want. Excuses are superfluous; fear-based; illogical; merely fabrications. They're stories we tell ourselves to make things so or not so. Remember, we are the creators. We can have anything we want, and excuses not to attain what we want should never direct us.

Since we give ourselves no excuses, we deal with logic alone. Logic takes the threads of opposites and binds them together into an overview. *Logic is the overview* of any situation; what leads us in the direction that serves 'the whole.' Logic sees directions, the 'yes' and the 'no,' and it may choose, but it *does not deviate from the overview*. Logic knows where it's going and how it's going to end up. Logic is a stance of power. Thus, we begin to enter *the heart way*. Our heart begins to give us instruction at that moment. Our intuition then guides us, because *the heart way is the intuitional way*. We have to choose what we want. We have to slow down our life enough to decide what we want, without excuses. Excuses are formed from mental attitudes; habitual energy.

We are preparing now to enter into the heart, itself. That's where we're going, aligning ourselves so that we can enter into our heart. This *Heart Sutra* makes us ready to enter the inner sanctum of that heart. In order to do that, we have to define what it is that we want. If we define it, we'll materialize it, through acceptance of that definition. We will see that everything can come to pass if we accept responsibility for what we want and move towards it. We are the only ones in the way. *Nothing else is in the way*. We get out of our own way by saying what we want without excuses, and then accepting responsibility for receiving it, and it will come to pass.

Our heart demands us to be true to ourselves. This puts us in a position of fulfillment. All our lives, we've wanted to be able to have exactly what we wanted. Okay, here it is. What we decide, unless *we* make it impossible, will come to pass.

We can see now why we can't be under the control of someone else's desires, and we can't be under the control of our own desires, because if we're under control of *desire of any kind*, then we can't have what we want, because desires are *before us*, reaching for something that's not there. Desire, by its nature, cannot be fulfilled, and if we think we have fulfilled it, notice the dissatisfaction that follows. Instead, what we want out of life is an ingredient that *must come from our own hearts*, which is quite different than desire.

What we truly want out of life contains the dharma, the primordial nature itself. It's the plus and the minus being brought together from the overview. Logic decrees that we should have what we want. It's *illogical* for us to live a life that we do *not* want, for any excuse. Excuses are nothing; remember, they're just like a puff of smoke, or a cloud, or a bubble.

It's a big responsibility to decide what we want, rather than 'wishing' for something; wishing is wishy-washy. Instead, we say we want something. *This is what I want out of life.* This has nothing to do with a 'wish,' nothing to do with desire. Desire arises from our lower self. We are talking about what our *heart* resonates with, the *true resonance* of our heart.

Money and other material things are energy; how do we relate to those energies? If we have such a concern about producing money, then logic decrees we have some kind of limitations about how we view that energy.

The creator cannot be biased. We can like things and not like things, but we'll know that we like it because we've developed a taste for it, and we'll not like it because we haven't developed a taste for it.

What keeps us back from what we want are *ideas* that tarnish our choices. We have notions about the energy that produces our choices. This is what holds us back, notions.

If we can give up attachment to all notions, our ideas of things, because such ideas about things are only fabrications from our own karma, then we would be free to receive. Fabrications from our own karma frequently tell us that we can't have what we want, because that's the way our karma is now set up. Otherwise, we wouldn't be wanting it; we'd already have it. See the logic there? Spirituality is the dharma, which runs along the avenues of logic.

We have to take a look at what we want. We have to let loose, not examine, the notions that we have, because if we examine the notions that we have, we're reinforcing them with excuses for their existence. Instead, we let go of our notions; in other words, *we approach something with a sense of emptiness*. It's only in that way that the heart is able to function intuitively. Notions undermine our sense of what it is we want. They are hidden feelings that don't allow us to have what we want. Instead, we approach what we want with no excuses whatsoever, without worry, because truly, if we are *properly aligned* with what we want, all of life will benefit.

Properly aligned means that whatever we want will bring happiness and fortunate conditions. Improper alignment creates unfortunate conditions. People may accumulate vast fortunes, yet be unhappy, like a fellow who wins the lottery and loses all his friends, because they now ask him for money, and his unfounded belief is that they now only want his friendship for his money. Notions about money caused problems. The 'good fortune' that brought him that money came from his giving to others in a previous life, but he gave for return. He felt entitled to receive for what he gave. So through a great deal of giving to get favors in return, he received rewards in an offhanded way. *What goes around comes around.* His wife took a big chunk of his winnings, then left him, and his friends did that, too, because he approached his friends, giving to them only to gain their friendship in return, so his giving was to get, not to truly give, which is unconditional. We are talking about wanting something that is going to bring *happiness.*

We have notions, ideas of what we think it is to get something, and we have to let go of those. We have these ideas set in our mind, which are nearly always incorrect, about what it is to get what we want. If it was so, we'd already have what we wanted, since having what we *want* is directly related to its fulfillment; but we don't. We have to let go of the notions in order to really *get it*, in spirituality.

What terrifies people is to be completely vulnerable to what they want, because even if they want money that will bring happiness, they have to be completely vulnerable to it and its existence in their lives. We have to open ourselves; otherwise, what we want won't bring happiness. It'll just be money that's earned in the market place or connived in some way, and it will bring unhappiness, bad karma, unfortunate circumstances, because of the kind of mentality that earned it. But, if we develop a mentality of openness, and we're completely vulnerable to that openness, then we have no notions about it. We want, and we'll be guided intuitively through the heart to go towards what we want, and happiness results.

This business of acting solely 'to be liked' by others is foolishness, because it becomes giving with conditions attached to it, which is not heartfelt. When we act in a heartfelt manner, we *give of ourselves.*

Here

in this glorious place known as Skycliffe,

we gather to put aside all things

for the sake of realizing

that without burdens and limitations,

items of personality,

we inherit ALL.

So, we're here for the express purpose to put aside all things and express our spiritual priority, intuitively knowing this is the only way we can enter this *Heart Sutra*....Here we stand, naked within ourselves, without excuses for functioning *for* or *against* anything, so that we can come to the *Heart* of *realization*.

Burdens and limitations are items of personality. All things that we consider burdensome, or we consider troublesome, or we consider that we can't do something because of false conditions or fears, such limitations are all items of reflected personality. If we can put these aside, the tides turn so that we inherit everything we want.

This doesn't mean that we cease to function as a personality in the world. It simply means that we put aside our grasping and our conviction that our burdens and our limitations, and other characteristics of personality, are real. Instead, *we live in the world, but not of it.*

At this stage, the task is to keep the excuses subdued, which are all bundles of feelings of burden and complications; a jillion complications of why we can or can't have something displayed as limitations set by our personality. This done, we easily see that personality is formulated by unfortunate karmic traits.

Such unfortunate traits express notions and ideas, confinements to our perceptions. Perceptions broaden when we see things for what they are—as manifestations of our own consciousness. We only *feel* we can't have what we want because of the multitude of excuses, which we deem to be reasons we display in our life, because these are what our consciousness manifests for us to see by mirroring the personality as we function in the world.

In truth, we are divinity in a body, looking out of the body and operating within the life that we have chosen for ourselves. We can make changes in any way we want and have anything we want, but when we focus on ourselves as a personality, we *depict* likes and dislikes, ideas and notions about things, and these limit us as burdens and limitations that we drag around as though we are chained to them.

Anytime we give ourselves an excuse for something, we owe it to ourselves to look deeply and make a note of that excuse, until we see such reason is nothing more than a fabrication of our personality, its way of viewing life. All excuses are fabrications of personality telling us we <u>have</u> to live a certain way.

Perceptions, backed by *excuse*, are based upon what we have learned, what we have heard, what we have been taught; composites of fabrications or distorted reality. Even knowing this, we still may be hesitant to drop any one of them, because we don't know who we are without such fabrications. In a manner of speaking, they make us feel safe in the discomfort they produce, because we are accustomed to them. They reflect our mental habits.

Being a spiritual student, *we must not 'typeset' ourselves,*...and if we have already 'typeset' ourselves, we should stop reading novels all together for awhile—for awhile, not forever. It is the same for a romantic, who listens to romantic music all the time; they 'typeset' themselves. Their minds become geared to what is heard. If we stop listening to that romantic music for a time,...when we go back to it, we'll see what it did to us.

Such sentimental journeys draw emotional responses, and we suffer sensations of feelings about loss and gain, all dual aspects of personality and karma. Emotional love is all about *self*. When we can learn to tune into the heart, however, get past the holds of personality, we will still use personality, but we'll do it with conscious awareness so that it doesn't rule us. We get past that, and we come to learn what the heart is *really* about. The heart is a powerful and reliable instrument, as we are about to find out, very powerful indeed.

Operating beyond personality requires spiritual wakefulness. We have to be able to see traits of personality and personality mental habits as they take us over and begin to lead us in *unwanted* directions. To actually see where it's taking us means we have come to recognize what personality is. Personality is built on emanations of disposition—characteristics and mental tendencies that develop as a result. Divinity will *make use* of going in one direction or the other, but it doesn't ever fall prey to being *unconsciously unaware* of those tendencies. Divinity, as consciousness, is very, very agile...because it can see where everything is going in the directions that it chooses to go, because life is a series of situations. That's what inventing our life is about. We make a series of situations. Because divinity can see this, it manages these from an overview, like a puppeteer plays with puppets on a stage.

So, this personality, if not operated by conscious awareness, is a troublesome character. The face in the mirror, depicting personality, is not a real face. It is a reflection. Unconscious personality, because it functions only from fabrication, is a reflection of karma, the type that brings about unfortunate conditions in a person's life. While karma is necessary for life, unfortunate karma can be kept at a minimum by being consciously aware of karma as it arises and diminishes. We have to portray a personality in order to be alive. The trick is to spiritually awaken so that we can see that we are portraying a personality, and to use it consciously, rather than unconsciously let *it* take charge of us. *We, as divinity, master it, not let it master us.*

Personality lives like a character in a book. If it makes good sense that we're acting in a certain way, it means we're following a course that make sense to us. Such reasoning implies that we are attached to an aspect of life being a certain way. Unconscious behavior from a personality actually cloaks divinity—our true nature. When personality leads our consciousness, our awareness is limited, and we fall spiritually asleep.

When such an established personality is in power, divinity becomes dormant. Remember, divinity is the inspirational spark that keeps us alive, not personality. Personality can't keep us alive. When strong fear, strong hatred burns a course to keep us alive, such burning force makes our bodies sick, and causes misery, suffering, and loneliness—the body, mind, spirit connection is broken.

Divinity, our true nature, is our real protector, the giver and creator of life, but it can only protect life, our life, when we allow it to operate our personalities.

The ego says it can defy mind-sets and force an outcome through willful execution, but this is not true. The only way to deal with mind-sets is *by yielding to divinity.* If we try to deal with mind-sets through the personality, then those mind-sets are under the personality's charge, and the personality is the creator and maker of the mind-set.

Thus, we cannot enter the heart just yet, because the heart intuitively can't relate knowledge to us as long as the personality is in command. Reasons, excuses really, close off intuition. Intuition is much more than just a little hunch. Intuition is a tremendous power.

The *Heart Sutra* takes us in a direction that is quite enormous. To prepare ourselves, we have to see from the overview what type of patterning we've run our life by. What kind of reasons do we give ourselves? Ego talks about worthiness or unworthiness, righteousness or unrighteousness....It likes to grandstand in those arenas. That kind of grandstanding portrays all sorts of prideful situations, or 'un-prideful' situations. Pride and feelings of unworthiness are traits of ego. Obsession is a destroyer. The wisdom of divinity can never get through to us as long as the mind is poisoned by anger, lust, greed, vanity, and attachment.

Expressions of Emotions (Mind Poisons) from Habitual Mind

Expressions from Divine Overview

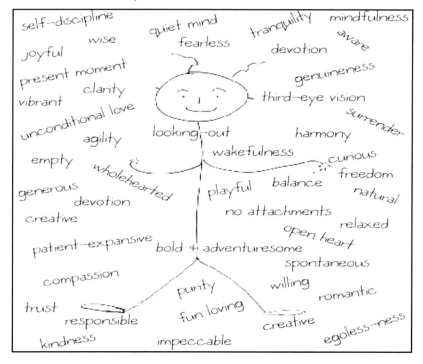

self-discipline
wise
joyful
present moment
clarity
vibrant
unconditional love
agility
empty
wholehearted
generous
devotion
creative
patient-expansive
compassion
trust
responsible
kindness

quiet mind
fearless
looking-out
wakefulness
playful
bold & adventuresome
purity
fun loving
impeccable

tranquility   mindfulness
aware
devotion
genuineness
third-eye vision
surrender
harmony
curious
freedom
balance
natural
no attachments
relaxed
open heart
spontaneous
willing
romantic
creative
egoless-ness

When divinity animates karma to life, that great good karma that it's fashioned from then responds in the world through the giving of service that nurtures the *whole*. The responder, in this case, is the divinity—refined personality. Our bodies are divinity's vessels. In order to have that vessel function perceptively, it has to access favorable imagery. Divinity makes use of mind and body so that it can function in the world.

So here we are a karmic unit. Our body, mind, and spirit are functioning according to the karma we are carrying within us. Our evolvement, or lack of it, dictates how we live life. But, if we start to spiritually awaken, if we start to become aware of this fact, then we begin to consciously evolve, so that nothing is in the way to receive whatever it is that we want. We'll not have any mental quirks in the way for us to *receive*, and no quirks in the way for us to *give*.

If we want a friend in life, our friend will mirror the conditions of our karma. Everything we have in our lives mirrors our karma. So, if we are obsessive, our obsessiveness is a reflection of our karma. There is no such thing as a 'magnificent obsession.' *Never*. There's nothing magnificent about obsession, which, by its nature, is lustful. Obsession, birthed from lust, is an addiction.

So the reasons we give ourselves for the way our life has unfolded in a certain way also 'mirror images' our karma.

Now, we're beginning to see how life operates. *When true knowledge is given to us, we have a responsibility to make use of it.* If we don't, our ignorance is magnified. We make unfortunate situations for ourselves through living ignorantly. If we know something is incorrect, and we insist on living in such old, ignorant patterns, then we're bringing ourselves to a place of great suffering and unfortunate conditions.

So this is our responsibility: When we begin to spiritually awaken, and we begin to learn spiritually, we have a responsibility to make use of what we learn by actually putting what we learn into practice in our lives. If we claim that it's not convenient at a particular time to put such knowledge to work in our life, because we want something in an obsessive way, we're going to suffer, because this is what brings suffering to us.

We have to take a look at the excuses we give ourselves. Such reasoning will reveal the pattern of lifestyle that we have been living in this lifetime. It shows us the *illusion* we're living through, and the *delusion* we are also living through.

All along, we have been a personality, a composite of reasoning that has set a pattern, and the pattern played out is called a personality. We need to take a step further, so that we can progress *through* this illusion that has been binding us to free us to traverse *the way of the heart*.

Personality,

having no real self-substance,

devises creations that are based on sensations,

perceived by miniscule viewpoints,

and tied together by likenesses that evaporate

like droplets of water in hot air.

If, however,

we realize this, we can instead,

use personality as a Divine Tool.

One of the most interesting aspects of spiritual awakening is, the more a person awakens, the grander their sense of humor becomes. This occurs because personality lacks the substance of true self and, instead, relies on reasons or causes, which are not divinity, and therefore, not free for playful, paradoxical interactions. Being illusionary by nature, personality is built on causation.

Personality views life by dividing objectivity from subjectivity and, as a result, becomes fascinated by pinpricks of viewpoints to postulate understanding: "Oh, I know what an elephant looks like," just by viewing from pinprick sight. "I know what the sky is like," and all they see is the surface of the sky and determine its nature from its surface, which is illogical.

All that is truly known from this perspective is what already appears familiar, 'miniscule viewpoints.' The *miniscule viewpoint* is that we only know something by how it is *familiar* to us. By its familiarity, we recognize it, but beyond that, we don't really know it. We just know what part is *familiar to us*, which describes the miniscule viewpoint.

Now, we have broadened our spheres with the computer age and being able to travel from one continent to another in a day's time. The world seems smaller, and it appears we have vast knowledge of the world, but such knowledge is *still* from a miniscule viewpoint.

The miniscule viewpoint is the viewpoint of personality. This personality, that is a composite of reasons and elaborations of excused behavior, goes out into the world, looks at the world, and says, "Oh, I know what all this is about," because it recognizes faces. Many faces bear resemblances. Everywhere we go, we see with familiarity, but such familiarity is *still* merely viewing from the surface.

We see countries in the news, so we think we know about that country, but all we *really* know is what the news is telling us. What we know is surface knowledge, lacking experience, so it's a miniscule viewpoint. Even if we visit another country, we only experience the part of it we touch.

The personality sees things through its own karma. The personality sees things not as they are, but through the causes and effects that formed its idea of self-identity.

To have a broader viewpoint, we have to be able to wake up to that place where *we are divinity operating the personality*. We operate a personality *propitiously* to fit the instant that we're dealing with. Divinity operates a personality in such a way that *whatever the moment calls for...that is what is given*.

Divinity never operates unconsciously from habit. It would be impossible for it to do so. The nature of divinity is agile. It can juxtapose positions; it can expand its viewpoint to see everything all at once. It sees the causes which operate situations, and it will *use* the personality to function as a tool within a situation, but then shift into a direction that is broader.

When we use personality 'as a divine tool,' we function within the world, *interpreted* as a personality by other apparitions we come in contact with, but we are not that. We are divinity wearing a physical body. All apparitions of sentient form are divinity wearing a physical body. We are apparitions of karma, and, of course, either conscious, or unconscious, creations of that karma. We operate within this world of causation, but we're not of the world. *We live in the world, but we do not enter the oblivion of its delusion.*

Societies of the world, cultures of the world, are built on reasons, excuses for situations and responses. That's why there is a culture; tradition comes from this. A society or a culture is likened to a personality. Religions each have a personality; governments each have a personality. If we work within a government agency successfully, we adopt its personality. That is what denotes success. We live happily in a country, and we feel like it's home, because we have adopted the traditions of that country. We have adopted the personality of that country.

Everything that we like in life and everything that we dislike in life has personality to it. If we dislike it, it's because we're in conflict with that personality, and if we like it, it means that we are accepting of that personality. If it has a mystique to us, it's because that personality has made us curious. It's something that is part of us, but not part of the way that we normally live, that we'd like to find out about.

What is this mystique? It's actually our divinity. It's what draws us like a magnet. We look at something and it has a mystique to it, so naturally that means we know there is that quality in us, but we can't see how to place it, how to live it yet. That's *why* it's a mystique.

This is how one begins on the spiritual path, seeking; and then we give ourselves to what we're seeking. We gain that trust. Slowly, trust begins to build up through our experiences, and we develop trust in this manner. In the beginning, when we have no trust, we cannot walk the spiritual path. The heart is stone-closed as far as we believe 'give enough, but don't give too much.'...There's a 'closed-ness.' In any situation, one gives just so much. *The awake heart lives in an open state and does not measure giving and receiving.*

After we realize this personality and how it drives all physical life, we become aware that we live in the world, yet we are not of it.

Seeing things as plus or minus, 'good' or 'bad,' is limiting, because 'good' means there's a reason for goodness—usually points of view, rather than logic—and 'bad' means there's a reason for badness. Using the thread of dharma or logic to view life, we view life from an overview. When we do this, then we are aware of the personalities of things. We can move along and be comfortable in what would otherwise be uncomfortable situations, because we realize that we don't have to have been biased to feel comfortable.

If we're operating our purpose in life through our divinity, then we are operating our personality *consciously.* Our personality, then, becomes *an extension or expression of our divinity.*

As a Divine Tool,

personality is freed within the Great Ocean.

Its talents then rise up from unfathomable depths...

from within the sacred sea.

Then,

whenever rapture between Heart and Purpose connect,

the cause is complete, and

the Prajna clears.

In this stanza, we are still preparing for the *Heart Sutra*. *Prajna* refers to consciousness. So we're using personality as a divine tool, rather than personality running rampant according to the reasons in life it perceives.

The *sacred sea*, the *Great Ocean,* is Divinity itself, the Void, of which we are a part....Many people refer to the Void as God. *God is without personality*, so we're not giving it an identification of a personality, instead, we're saying it is the Great Ocean or the Void.

The heart is an accessible depth within the Great Ocean. All talents arise from the Great Ocean, and *the Great Ocean and the heart, while not exactly alike, are somewhat synonymous.* This *heart* content, intuition, makes it inseparable from the Void. So, personality becomes freed within the Great Ocean, and its talents within the Great Ocean become usages to uplift other persons, to live for the good of the whole.

In this position, when freed within the Great Ocean, persons can only function living for the good of the whole, which is divine love and compassion. Here, we cannot do anything that would be termed 'for excuse' or 'self-centeredness.' All action is always for the good of the whole, or always uplifts other life forms whenever we act from within this Great Ocean. Its talents are all connected to the upliftment of others.

We then also realize that we are not our bodies, but we know that in order to make use of life, we need body as a physical vessel. So, we take very good care of our body, and we are respectful of its needs. We don't ask it to engage in obsessiveness of any kind. We don't engage in the mind poisons (anger, lust, greed, vanity, or attachment), so therefore, the body is not poisoned either, because when the mind is poisoned, the body is poisoned.

Here in this place, within this Great Ocean, the talent arises to be able to give more, to be more vulnerable.

Within the Great Ocean, because we are divinity and we know that we're the creators, we make ourselves completely vulnerable, without definition....The word 'completely' will mean without defining any way of being vulnerable; without definition, we are completely vulnerable. We live life so openly that we're vulnerable, but in that vulnerability, in that openness, the personality can be useful for the upliftment of life, and it facilitates in the creation of life.

When we're living within this sacred sea,...*rapture between heart and purpose connect*....This ecstatic movement of rapture occurs when we unify with the heart. Subject and object are unified, so they're inseparable at that point.

The personality then becomes an extension of this Great Ocean.... '*Whenever rapture between heart and purpose connect*,' the heart meaning this Great Ocean of *love and purpose connect*. Here we are referring to a divine love, unconditional love; it has nothing to do with emotion. Divine love encompasses compassion, which is unrelated to emotion. Emotion is relative to (mind/feelings) memory-passions: anger, lust, greed, vanity, and attachment, and all the little derivatives that would be listed under those categories. (*See Chart, pg. 36*)

Emotions that are carried around in life as attitudes are mind poisons. Remember, mental poisons result in body poisons. They are the cause of ill health. The causation and self-reflective feelings that are centered around these mind poisons cause the physical body to suffer....Thought processes that we use in situations in life will also make the suffering for us, because of the existence of these mental poisons.

Mental poison distorts and pollutes. It brings unwanted sensations, unfavorable conditions, ill fortune.

Mind poisons are what people call emotions, and of course, they can never be healed. *We cannot heal an emotion.* We cannot cure ourselves of anger. We cannot cure ourselves of lust. We cannot cure ourselves of attachment. We simply have to adopt this divine viewpoint, or alchemy, which then transmutes the poison through our awareness. We do this through the practice of mindfulness, or awareness that we are aware of every innuendo of feeling and thought, how they connect, and the driving forces that we have, the reasons that we give ourselves. When we can see all situations starting to play out in our lives, *we have experienced mindfulness*, and when we become *adept* at it, then we have become adept at *Third Eye Vision*, and when we become adept at that, then we *become unified* with the Great Ocean.

So, *whenever unity between heart and purpose connect*, the cause is complete, and *Prajna* clears. The consciousness becomes *divine*. *Prajna* refers to consciousness.

Now, we're beginning to learn a little bit about the heart. We know the heart cannot be separated from the Great Ocean. So, the heart is not the bearer of emotions after all. People always look at the heart as the bearer of emotions, but the bearer of emotions would be the bearer of mind poisons—anger, lust, greed, vanity, and attachment, and all those little feelings that come under it. (*See Chart, pg. 36*)

Emotions are negative imprints of karma, *negative* because they form chaos. They make us feel trapped. We think we have to live a certain way because of our identification with emotions, which is not so.

No reason, as an excuse, is logical because logic is an overview, not a division or segment of an overview. Something might seem reasonable, and still not be logical. Logic is a combination of the plus and the minus of a situation, the positive and the negative, combined to assume a third element, the whole or unity of a thing or situation.

Through our attention, we create. When we remove our attention, our involvement dissipates, and what we have created declines.

In this same sense, as we develop awareness of habits arising, the mental play that is so familiar to us about them then falls away. Everything will fall away that is *not* bound by our attention. This is an important fact in life. As creators, we have to know the way to create is through our attention. When heart and purpose unify through rapture, unification, creation is effected.

We need to take a look at the habitual mind-plays that go on inside of us *as they are playing out* in order to truly be mindful. Awareness, which is the result of mindfulness, makes us very inwardly quiet throughout the day, because every time we look at something, we see a flash, a memory of some kind. We don't have to intercept it, only see it as it arises. If we give something our attention, it will remain. If we remove our attention, it will dissolve.

As we walk around in a state of awareness, we observe whatever arises. If we don't focus our attention on what arises, but merely proceed on our way, what was seen dissolves. To become aware of that instant of dissolution is *very, very* important, just as it is to be aware of what is created. This wouldn't be important if we weren't creators. But because we are creators, we actually manifest life through our attention; therefore, we need to be aware of the high points of our attention. When our attention is fastened on something, it brings circumstances about, and when the attention is not fastened on something, it dissolves.

If we have a problem, and we look deeply, with our attention on the problem, the problem is magnified. That's what attention does; it magnifies. It brings a little *seed body* of something that exists into magnification, so it manifests into greater and greater scenarios around us.

We manifest our lives in this way—through our attention; and our attention comes about through our attraction or repulsion to things. If we are repulsed by something, our attention is very strongly fastened on it....By being repulsed, we become personal with what repulses us, and, as a result, we will be overcome by it.

If we see ourselves as creators, which means we are willing to take responsibility for our circumstances, we feel ready to make necessary or chosen corrections and changes.

As such, in samsara,

the Divine Tool whispers intuitively.

Whatever needs to be known is known,

including situational directions,

any knowledge of existence—both sentient and non-sentient—

as well as life and death.

As such refers to: *Then, whenever rapture between the heart and purpose connect, the cause is complete, and the Prajna clears.* Once we come to this place of rapture between heart and purpose, and they connect, the consciousness clears so that our divinity is the captain of our lives.

When our divinity is in the driver's seat, *the Divine Tool whispers intuitively.* The divine tool, which is divinely integrated personality, is now united with the heart; it no longer is controlled by likes and dislikes, nor with notions or attitudes. It can make use of those characteristics, but it is now a divine tool. It has united with the heart. Anything about life and death is then revealed to us in this state. When divinity is exposed and we're living *as* divinity, then anything we need to know is opened unto us, because there isn't any obstruction to make anything unknown. If something is unknown, our *awareness* is not available at that moment, and so we lack the *ability* to give it our attention. If there's no obstruction, anything that we need to know is there. It's that simple.

Personality is freed within the Great Ocean. Its talents then rise up from unfathomable depths, from within the sacred sea. Then, whenever rapture between Heart and Purpose connect, the cause is complete, and the Prajna clears.

Such connection at a certain point is eminent and *constant*. Everything we come in contact with, we connect to. Our heart and purpose connect; all things within our sphere of attention make a constant connection through the openness we have established in ourselves. When there are no mind passions, there is only openness. When openness comes about, then rapture is present because the unification of heart and purpose has come about, and the consciousness is freed to be its natural identity. Its natural identity, of course, is divinity. Living life in this way, we use the divine tool. We then use the personality in our life situations, and...*it is not using us.* Our full awareness and our consciousness is open to the knowledge that we are using karmic talents *by choice.* We choose to do this, and we choose not to do that.

When we make a conscious choice, we use the divine tool. We know that, if we don't make choices, life will make choices for us. So, we use the divine tool, rather than not use it, which is wisdom. Wisdom makes use of the divine tool. If we don't make use of it, then we become victim to whatever circumstances exist that we have materialized in the past and that other sentient forms have materialized in the past without our choice. Even when we manifest situations for ourselves, what we manifest constantly changes. Once something manifests, it becomes less and less of its original nature, unless it becomes more and more of itself from our constant attention.

If we remove our attention from something purposefully, what we had manifested will fall apart. This is something a recluse comes to realize, and they feel free when their outward manifestations cease to exist. We, who are living *in* life, *consciously* manifest. If what we have manifested serves the whole, because we're living as divinity, then we maintain its existence through our attention on it. We maintain existence through our attention. We have to always have some degree of attention on it; otherwise, whatever we manifest becomes weakened.

It begins in this way...

All phenomena are seen as indications

and assertions,

which means it is empty of entity.

Even though the heart pumps blood to sustain the body, and

the spirit prompts the mind,

no entity is present, only containers of energy.

Thus,

the Prajna is free of controls and, instead,

responds from clairvoyant choice.

All phenomena are seen as indications and assertions. All manifestations of all kinds are seen as indications and assertions. *They are indications of energy...and assertions of mind.* Mind is not an entity. Mind is a projector of feeling, intention, or rapture and purpose—*images* reflected onto the *universal mind screen* onto what we refer to as the *environment.* Such environment refers to all we perceive around us—the natural and structural environs— places where we live, work, and play. Our *usage* of mind *portrays* karma as entities, and these determine karma to be our personality and the personalities that we interact with. This means that *all phenomena are seen as indications and assertions*, which means that they are empty of entity. *All phenomena are empty of entity.* Although we see ourselves as an entity, what we see is karma, a personification of likes and dislikes, attitudes and opinions, but

50

there is no entity there. When we use it in the way of making choices, it appears like it is an entity, but in reality, the entity is not there. The entity that is really showing itself is the *wakefulness of divinity, portrayed as* consciousness, or *consciousness wrapped with karma,* through which it assumes identification. The body is a manifestation of karma; therefore, it is a part of the phenomenal or, so-called, manifested world. It is empty of entity. It is brought to life, asserted to life, actually, *through divinity.*

When divinity is able to shine through, this means the *prajna* or consciousness has its awareness intact. In this manner, while we still operate with karma, we consciously, with awareness, know that we are now acting something out. Because we know this, we don't get caught up in the attitudes and opinions that insist on acting out *in a certain way.* There's no compulsion to make it so, and no obsession to drive it. This is the difference. Such compulsive, obsessive being is a fabricated entity....It's an apparition that is fashioned by karma. It's a 'phantom being' that actually looks and responds to karma and nothing else. It has no *true* free will. *We have free will as divine beings,* but karma has no free will. Karma is not an entity, so it has no free will. Karma is just something that has accumulated through action-reaction, a cause of physics,...so it responds in a certain way: action-reaction-action....It always goes in cycles, and the cycle of three is...there's an action; we have a reaction, and we make another reaction out of the first two. We drive reactions obsessively and compulsively. When reactions occur, we have compulsion to make certain movements or certain decisions in a likeness or unlikeness way, to act out whatever role it is we're playing in a certain situation in a certain way. We have this *process* that we live by, and in that process, that's how we see things and do things, and it's all driven by karma.

When we look around and see how life is constructed, we can

see that, without us, life cannot exist. Our karma fashions our lives because we perpetuate it by the made-up pictures that we live in. We do that from all the mental imagery that we carry. When we spiritually awaken, we will still see mental imagery...but with *awareness to avoid unnecessary suffering*....When we start to pick and choose things that are uplifting to ourselves, then we realize that because they *are* uplifting to us, they are also uplifting to all others, as well. When we realize this, then we create *more consciously*, forgetting about the karmic baggage that's been weighing us down for thousands of years, and we begin to create, and *enjoy* being creators, in a life of service. Creation, then, becomes all about love and compassion. Nothing else matters at that point....*The body can constantly feel this love that flows through it.* It's an actual body sensation. It's very potent, and *that's* what heals our bodies. This is really and truly what the healing is that takes place in our bodies....This love flow becomes so strong; our vitality becomes strong, and our bodies stay healthy because of it. It can also give us the capacity to heal *others,* as well as *ourselves*, but such healing in others doesn't last unless such others can learn to maintain health.

We heal ourselves, and in doing so, we can also heal others, but it's useless to heal others' *dis*-ease, since they will quickly take it back on again. Better that they *learn* that *they are the creators*, and how to heal themselves. What makes a person sick is *mind poison*. They carry around these images, and they churn them, and churn them, and churn them. These memories 'churn, churn, churn,' and it breaks down their vitality. When a person starts to wake up, they start to take control of their lives, and they take control of their health. Becoming the conscious creator is a tremendous step....Free will is *total power,* but such power can only operate for the good of the whole. It's the only thing that it's capable of. *It can't do anything else.* If there was any other intention involved, it would have to be part of mind passions, so it couldn't exist. There can be no fear in free will, which is a statement of logic. Free will cannot co-exist with fear, because fear is contrary to the existence of free will.

As creators, we are divinity wearing bodies, and when we truly wake up to that, we can live with full intention from that knowledge. It is our *birthright* to do so, and since it *is* our birthright, know also, that it is our *responsibility* to do so. Since it is our birthright *to awaken to the divinity that we are*, then we know it is also our responsibility.

Listen!

Intuition cannot exist without free will.

In this way, the mind has not been transferred (to an entity),

and the objects of transference

have not arisen.

In a mirror, when the reflection of a face appears,

it appears without a face, the reflection being transferred

from face to object ... like dreams in sleep;

like waves, which are the nature of water;

rivers flowing in four directions

are the same in the ocean.

In moments that we tap into our divinity – and this happens sporadically throughout a non-awakened person's life – there are flashes of intuitive knowledge. Such knowledge comes from free will, because *free will* is a part of the anatomy of *divinity*. Intuition cannot exist without free will. Divinity cannot be bound, and it cannot be limited. It can only exist through free will.

*In this way, the mind has not been transferred, and the objects of transference have not arisen.....*The explanation is, *In a mirror, when the reflection of a face appears, it appears without a face.* When we look into a mirror, we see a face, but it really appears as a reflective device. There is not a 'face' there, only a *reflection. In this way, the mind has <u>not</u> been transferred to an entity.* The mind *cannot* be transferred to an entity. There is no entity; there are only reflections....*And the objects of transference have not arisen*....The face has not arisen. *In a mirror, when the reflection of a face appears, it appears without a face, the reflection being transferred from face to object...like dreams in sleep,* which explains the nature of dreams....like a face appearing in a mirror. *Like waves, which are the nature of water, rivers flowing in four directions are the same in the ocean.* If we put four rivers, each flowing in four directions into the ocean, how would they be distinguished? Likewise, when discussing the *prajna consciousness,* which is free from controls, it responds from clairvoyant choice.... *Intuition cannot exist without free will.* Where does intuition come from? It comes from divinity. The heart is the place where intuition resides. When we say the heart or intuition is 'synonymous' with divinity, this does not mean that divinity has a *location*, rather, it has a *heart*. It has a *knowing center*....It's like the river that's going in four directions within the great ocean.

The heart knows everything. It's not the heart in the physical body that we're talking about, although this is a physical manifestation of the same principle, the same thing that we're discussing. As a physical manifestation, the heart pumps blood in all directions; it pumps cellular energy; it pumps life in all directions. All knowledge comes from this *knowledge center*, which is *intuition*, which is *the heart of divinity*....This heart has no boundaries to it, just like divinity has no boundaries to it. *Divinity is reality, and reality has no limitations.* In using logic, which is the only way we can even approach reality, we can see that divinity has no limitations whatsoever, and yet it has this heart center, this nature-of-knowledge center of all things. It is part of all that is, but what it is, this intuition, is *also logic*;...the answer itself that comes, will always appear as logic rather than opposites, dual energies, although it can advise us to go in a particular direction.

How do we enter into this place of intuition? Through *mindfulness*. It is the only doorway, because it is the doorway that leads us to Third Eye Vision....The only way that we can tap into divinity is through Third Eye Vision, and the only way we can consistently use intuition, or tap into knowledge consistently, is through the practice of mindfulness.

So what are we going to do with this information? We have to practice mindfulness with a purpose. Remember, when the *heart connects with purpose*, we're going to end up in a place that is going to lead us deeper and deeper into this *real* realm. We need to practice mindfulness. These aren't words just to be said....It's something to be *lived* every instant, every breath. We really have to *give* ourselves to mindfulness, to observe our mental imagery as it arises. Thus, our attention so engaged, we observe the invisible presence of feelings that would ordinarily arise from such imagery, which keeps it from manifesting to poison our attention.

To reach the depth that we're going to, if we're brave enough to go there,...we have to use our moments to develop mindfulness as we go. It's all right to slip and become distracted or absorbed in something, to forget; but even while watching a movie, we should practice mindfulness. Don't *think* about practicing mindfulness, because when we *think* about practicing mindfulness, we are *not* practicing mindfulness.

So...

Mind and primordial wisdom are like moisture

and its water;

is and is not demonstrate a mind

that is apprehending.

There is nothing to do, and no doer to do it.

By liberating

denial and assertions into the primordial,

happiness will be achieved.

Moisture would be the essence....*Mind* is like moisture, and *primordial wisdom* is like water. Both *is* and *is not* demonstrate *a mind that is apprehending*,...a mind that is capturing notions, trying to capture ideas of things. In truth, there is nothing to do, and no doer to do it. By liberating denial of this, or of anything, and assertions, or activity of some kind, into the primordial, happiness will be achieved...by accepting the fact that there is nothing to do and no doer to do it in all reality.

Yes, we are creators, so we have to learn to create, but as we are creating, what creating will teach us is *that there is no entity at all.* It will teach us that there's nothing to do, and there is no doer to do it. It will teach us to let go of notions and ideas of things. The more we create in life, the more we come to the realization of what is superficial and what is real. Yes, all actions were done to serve the whole, but *in the ultimate stage, the whole is truly served by this emptiness, and not by things.*"

So, not only is there *no deity*, there is *nothing to do* and there is *no doer*. But here we are, we're learning that we're creators, so we're learning that it's our responsibility not to have what we do *not* want in our life, as *The Invocation for a Happy Life** has taught us. (*Invocation for a Happy Life – A HÜMÜH prayer that evokes the divinity within oneself by teaching one about the tenets of a happy life.) *The Invocation for a Happy Life* is the foundation for one's initial Bodhisattva vow. It is the thing that we go back to and refer to again, and again, and again, because...it instructs how to live. It tells that if we live in this way, refined life results, and we can test this out. It has those truths, which if one lives by them, one will have the life that one wants.

Primordial wisdom can be likened to water. It is the *substance* itself, and *mind* is that *essence* of the primordial, if we are living in that manner. If we're living from our divinity, then mind projects that essence, the moisture from the water. The creator springs from our divinity. It's our divinity that manifests as creator, but one's divinity is no different from another's divinity. It is one in the same; it is not separate. It is the Great Ocean, meaning that it is One. We're not separate. We are separate in our karma, which means we're separate in our degree of wakefulness, but our divinity is exactly the same. It is not separate.

When we're learning to be the creators, we have to remember not to get caught up in or possessive of our creations. If we get caught up in our creations, immediately we fall into mind poisons, because we will believe the creations to be reality when they are only faces in the mirror. Mindfulness teaches us to remember that we are *not* the reflection. Mind is nothing but a *portrayer*. It *portrays* whatever essences are coming off of us as karmic beings. If that essence is primordial wisdom, then that's one type of portrayal, and if it's mind poisons or emotions, that's another type.

A physical being *is* solidified karma. *Spirit* is an impetus that arises from our divinity. It is a force, the force that comes from divinity. When we use the force consciously, we align primordially.... There are many ways of expressing the divine force....We use the force in our creations, and we use its spirit or essence in our creations.

All

deliberate concepts are fabrications.

If whatever arises, arises free

from conceptual reasoning,

it is Primordial Wisdom —

sudden purity Primordial Awareness.

The realization that results

is that the phenomenon of the world and beings,

are the naturally pure Buddha-Field.

All concepts are fabrications. All conceptual thoughts of any kind are fabrications, since thought, by its relative considerations, is by nature, fabricated. There is nothing that is conceptual, or in idea form, that is not a fabrication. This is not to say that ideas cannot be constructive; it's just to say that all ideas are fabricated for constuctiveness. They consist of illusionary properties that manifest in the physical realm. Any illusionary property is otherwise called *phenomena*. *All matter is phenomena*. All matter arises from conceptual fabrication. All matter arises from fabrications, from ideas.

Intuition arises free from conceptual reasoning....It arises from awareness...logic (knowing and intuition)...compassion. Divinity relates to phenomena as compassion because it is love, but at the same time, as it arises, it is free from concept, although it may assist in conceptual speculation.

When one who is spiritually awake makes movement or takes

action, it is a result of touching the phenomenal realm with awareness. Intuition or compassion arises because of something we see or come in contact with.

The paper on which the Teachings are printed is conceptual, the ink is conceptual, the color is conceptual, but the *comprehension* that comes from that is *not* conceptual. Such arising does not come from the paper or the ink. It *does* come from the choice of words, but choice energizes them in a non-conceptual way. The *choice* is an exercise of spirit or essence of mind that is portraying the mental images—enlightened or unenlightened.

Primordial Wisdom is *non-conceptual*; however, it can be applied conceptually. We can use mundane wisdom, but the wisdom aspect of the mundane is non-conceptual, in the same manner that compassion is non-conceptual.

There is a *sudden purity*; that purity is not tainted with concepts or ideas; it simply exists as it exists, without any dressing to it. The dressing is conceptual, which takes many forms. It is 'ornamented' by explanations: ideas of *this* versus ideas of *that*, and of how these things work together, the coming together of two things. But here, *the coming together* is something that primordially exists all by itself.

The Buddha-Field, which exists in the pure, intuitive heart, is Primordial Knowledge that says it 'knows,' and it 'knows' that it 'knows;' and it 'knows' because it is intuition pouring forth. *Intuition* that is pouring forth has no real characteristics to it, except that it *establishes relationship with whatever it touches.*

Anything we need to know in life, when we touch upon it *purely* without *any* conceptual notions, the answers pour forth. As soon as we have a speculation come up, or we weigh this against that...we are completely shut off and intuition cannot come through. But the moment that we put such reasons aside, there is just openness, that pouring forth from us as a vessel for divinity into another vessel for divinity. Then we are pure divinity. The objects that we are playing with in the physical realm—whatever we are operating with, one then knows what is to be done in the conceptual realm to *consciously* manifest what is needed.

As divinity in a human body, all we have to do is remove ourselves from mental poison to maintain a state of openness. This state will view the conceptual realm to work with it; however, concepts won't be the *primary* concern. Instead, we will be aware of the big picture of life itself, knowing that everything exists because we created thusly. Responsibility flourishes, but responsibility doesn't become a difficult stance to deal with. It is a place of pleasantness, actually. If we are creating something from this higher place within ourselves, then accepting responsibility is a place of pleasantness. If it nurtures the whole, it nurtures us.

We can't be separated from the whole. As soon as we separate from the whole, then the concepts of life are leading us into living a life focused on self. Such a life lacks awareness in that it lives conceptually, living only by ideas, obsession, and passion, which then creates an illusionary existence, filled with self-deceptive traps, rather than maintaining charge of our own life.

Life doesn't have to be filled with unpleasantries. When we get caught up in the conceptual ideas of things, we lose our perspective, we lose our overview, and we strive toward one direction or toward the other direction. What does 'striving' mean? Strife. *Logic is an overview of unity between opposites.* People believe 'suffering exists in the world' is a logical assumption. It is not logical; suffering is illogical. We can't find a point of logic that says it's logical that suffering exists. There is no such point of logic. Suffering exists because of mind poisons (anger, lust, greed, vanity, and attachment—*See Chart pg. 36*), not because of logic. It exists because of mind poisons, and that *is* logical....Logic cannot be found in illogical perceptions. If one is living in suffering, then their existence is illogical. They are living what they do <u>not</u> want, which is illogical and the cause of suffering....Such suffering has a root of karma attached to it, but as soon as that person starts to live as they <u>do</u> want, rather than as they don't want, then that stuff of negative karma begins to lose its solidness. Karma can't stay solid if we are living in *opposition* to the karma. Suffering results from an inner tug of war, a conflict within one's self, trying to go in two directions—trying to do what other people want us to do, and yet maintain our sense of our dreams of wanting something else. To live logically, one resides without conflict, because logic poses no duality. Only the *dual* aspects pose *conflict*. Therefore, logic is a place of no conflict; it unifies the duality. It's a place where we can see which direction to go in for a given situation. If we are living logically, we will live Primordial Wisdom; we are living from the overview, or from Third Eye Vision, which is the spawning place of Primordial Wisdom. The floodgates of knowledge with wisdom are open there, without conflict.

I am reminded of the story of the steward. It is the story of one of the lives of Sakyamuni before he became Buddha. In that life, he was a steward, or treasurer, to the king. He had a lovely wife at home, and his mother-in-law came over to visit the wife one day when he was at work with the king. She said to the wife, "You have such a good husband. He's so good he could be a really spiritual man. He might run off to live in the forest as a hermit." The wife says, "Oh, no, he wouldn't do that." But the mother keeps talking about it until the wife believes that it is quite possible and begins to believe in what her mother is saying....The neighbors hear her fears, and they discuss the possibility, as well, and they gather about the woman's house, now convinced that because the steward <u>is</u> such a good man, that he <u>will</u> run off to live in the forest, leaving his family behind. One day, the steward comes home from work, and all his neighbors are waiting for him outside saying, "Oh, you are going to become a hermit and live in the forest," and he answers, "No, I'm not. I'm not going to live in the forest." "Yes, yes, you are," the neighbors say. "You are such a spiritual man, you are going to be a hermit." In the end, their conviction that he was to be a hermit was so strong that he had to do it; otherwise, they would lose faith in the values he represented to them, which he believed in himself.

Similar stories play out for everyone at some point in their evolution. How can we say 'no' when we are asked to serve in that manner? We *can't*....We can stall for a couple of years, but eventually, we have to serve. That's why life positions us in this way. We position ourselves that way, because our divinity is ready to *move*, ready to *awaken*...ready to *serve*. We can't be happy at that point, unless we *can* serve. There's no purpose in maintaining a body, unless we can serve. The steward couldn't have gone back to the king and been the treasurer anymore. What would he be like? He would be empty...feeling unfulfilled and bored, and the king would tire of him. All his energies had gone out into life. He had a *pure* integrity, and that's why the people saw him in that manner. He had to follow through. It is a bold story.

Conceptual life itself cannot fashion Primordial Wisdom, but Primordial Wisdom can operate in the conceptual realm.

There will always be suffering in the world, which is stimulated by evolution. I didn't say '*and/or* de-evolution,' because de-evolution is really a part of evolution, from the overview. De-evolution *cannot* be the *end* result....When we see de-evolution *as evolution*, we see from the *overview*, because evolution then ceases to be a 'dual.' It then takes the shape of wholeness.

Life is illusionary, but the fact that life <u>can</u> exist is *Reality*. Seeing life from the overview, all components become *one*....*Divinity* is not a 'component' of life, it is what *makes life possible*; without it, there is no life. Through the existence of divinity, all things are possible. There are no limitations to divinity, so for anyone to say that they can't change their life because of *reasons* is absurd.

The Heart

beats purely in a Buddha-Field,

laced with dharma-thread.

Here, life is lived beyond the surface of the mirror

where ordinary life is usually lived.

This is an entrance into utter silence,

a realm where not a single thought is born.

When gazing outward from this agreeable place,

suddenly one forgets the gazing; all

objects disappear without a trace

and you can't even find your

own body. This is a time

when heaven

enters earth,

and earth enters heaven.

So, here we are in a Buddha-Field. Skycliffe,* in itself, is a Buddha-Field. It's laced with the *dharma-thread*. The dharma (primordial life-stream) holds Skycliffe together. Without the *dharma*, without the *divine consciousness*, that holds or weaves the *thread* through the land, it would be in the same kind of ordinary chaos that the rest of the world exists in.

*Skycliffe-HÜMÜH Monastery and Retreat Centre

Beyond the surface of the mirror, means that what makes a mirror, that which makes something reflect...is *beyond* the *surface* of the mirror. Beyond the reflection, to the reality of what constructs a mirror. A mirror, as we know, is a piece of glass that has some darkened, black background behind it...which holds the reflection and pushes the reflection out for us to see. In a place like Skycliffe, which is a Buddha-Field, we 'see' ourselves continuously. We are always confronted with our state of consciousness. A Buddha-Field is a place of unbiased consciousness.

When gazing outward from this agreeable place, suddenly one forgets the gazing; (the meaning of) all objects disappears without a trace and you can't even find your own body. This is a time when heaven enters earth, and earth enters heaven. This is meditation worth experiencing. In meditation, we arrive at that place where everything disappears; we are gazing outward into nothingness, and because we are looking into the nothingness, there is nothing. *We* don't even exist there anymore. There is a post-meditative state that follows that...the (inner) Buddha-Field extends *with* our attention. As our attention is 'lighted' on something, then it, too, becomes a part of that light consciousness that makes the Buddha-Field.

This is a time when heaven enters earth, and earth enters heaven....a bliss state whereby one feels *comfortable* in life....We can enjoy that emptiness inside of ourselves; we simply accept it; we don't strain. We are still on 'the approach' to the Heart Chamber. We cannot gain entrance into a place that is so *open* if we are *pushing* or *seeking* something. Seeking has a grasping, 'looking' quality to it which almost builds into a frenetic kind of thing. Seekers of the 'path' are always saying, "Oh, I have to figure *this* out, and I have to understand *this*, *that* and *the other thing*," which is grasping; we can't enter the heart in that manner. Instead, we allow ourselves to be *that* empty, so that we can *experience* 'emptiness.'

In the experience of emptiness, we will be able to enter the heart....the *divine* heart...the heart of God, the heart of divinity. But we have to stop straining for it....relax. There is nothing to search for. Seekers truly don't find anything until they stop seeking. Then they make a commitment to a direction and they learn about that direction. When they go as far as that direction will take them—and they should always go as far as that direction will take them—then they turn their attention outward again...to look for another direction that will take them further. This opening comes from us, when we're not grasping at anything.

In the place of true openness, we are in the center of the heart and we know everything. The only way to get to that place of knowing everything is to stop grasping at things. No push. No pull. There is *ease,* not difficulty. It's so easy. People become disturbed if anything is too *easy,* because they have been taught that gain comes from suffering. Gain comes when suffering *ends,* not before. That kind of simplicity can only lead us to the center of the heart. If it seems too simple, that means we are looking at the meaning of the words, and the words seem too simple; but the *experience,* in its simplicity, is truly elegant. Such words are merely guidelines. Each word is a little guidepost. Whenever we have any extra moments to ourselves, we need to take that time just to be open and quiet. Maybe with an eye of curiosity, or a state of being that's curious, but doesn't ask any questions. Just an 'openness' kind of curiosity, so that we can truly gain a sense of the *meaning* of openness.

Then...

whatever arises, be it strong desire, aversions, or

even pleasure over riches, represents

only the manifestation of the creative energy

of intrinsic awareness.

This is very much unlike the undercurrent of thoughts,

deriving unnoticed from mind, which

accumulates endless future karma

in the prison samsara.

Ordinary life, or *samsara*, would feel like a prison to one who has accessed the Heart, whenever they feel unable to live in a state of openness....As soon as they leave the openness, into a noisy, contrived mind, they instantly find themselves behind the bars. The only way to dissolve this feeling is to return to that place of *openness.* Therefore, it is very important that we indoctrinate ourselves in the *experience* of being *open,* whereby our attention sees everything and can be focused on one thing, yet it never *touches* anything. It is completely agile because it has no boundaries. We develop agility of attention, not *jumping* from one thing to another, yet there is the freedom to *move* without having actual *contact* with anything.

Our *attention* should be *like a ball of light suspended* in the air that can turn 360 degrees. This multiple attention *span* is graced with the ability of tracking energy and viewing the energies that approach or leave—agile and flexible—from spaciousness. Our goal is to develop this sense of spaciousness. We will then have experiences that moderate the karma we are operating—that will help us see a great many things. In such *seeing*, there will be *solutions* that arise. These solutions will arise from *divine reality**...because of the openness that our attention experiences.

(*The Three Realities: 1) The Void or God, 2) Divine Consciousness, which realizes the Void, and 3) Life, also called the dreamtime.)

From this place of attention—this ball of light in front of ourselves that we would call our attention—we have the distinct capabilities of seeing *past*, *present* and *future* as <u>now</u>. Ordinary consciousness cannot see that, it has to 'figure it out,' and as soon as it tries to figure it out, it loses its sense of that <u>now</u> in a myriad of conceptions and conceptual reasons. But to float the consciousness *unhindered*, the past, present and future are <u>now</u>, and it is clearly seen that way. There is no struggle in the attainment of this consciousness. It is one of the gifts that come to us from living in divine reality. Do remember, it's one thing to do something as 'an experience,' and it's another to do it as a 'committed way of life,' and therefore, become *one* with that. Being *one* with that, the gifts are much greater.

Mastery of attention begins with awareness, without grasping onto things with our attention. For example, as long as I hold my glasses, they are 'attached' to me in a physical way, yet my attention may not hold them. Instead, my attention may be *making use of* them, while not *holding* them; not *touching* them. We have to train our attention *not to touch*....We don't want anything *blocked-off*, so our attention cannot be touching. Our attention can only be *viewing*. It can be *open* in that viewing, but if it's *touching* something, then there is a part that is blocked-off by being grasped.

And grasping, of course, is attachment. That's why attachment is such a bearer of unfavorable karma. When we have an attachment to things, or people, and we *claim* things, we create unfortunate karma, because such grasping is *ownership by attention.* Our health is not negatively affected by the *things* we own; it is negatively affected by *what we grasp with our attention,* the latter being an effect of our emotions or mental poisons. When we can keep our attention 3 or 4 feet out in front of us...we are never attached to anything, and we are never *blinded* by our attachments. In this way, we can feel how attachments *blind* us, because whatever part of us is grasping is blind. To maintain health in body, mind and spirit, we don't let *things* or relationships in life *blind* us. We have them, we enjoy them, but we are not attached to them.....Our attention can be *on* them; it can see what needs to be done...to better a relationship, or to bring about wanted circumstances. It can focus *in* on that, but *it always keeps the peripheral awareness.* That's the *power* of the attention that's extended in that way.

What makes relationships difficult is when people have a *haunting* feeling inside that they can never leave. There should never be that kind of a feeling. If we are not attached, we can have a wonderful relationship, and we can *re-make* that relationship better and better through time, *if* we don't grasp or cling to the other person.

We have to learn to suspend our attention out in front of us. This will prepare us for entering this 'heart;' and prepare ourselves, we must, because it is the only way to gain entrance. There is no other way. Not only do we gain entrance into the heart of divinity, we gain a very golden memory that will grace our lives.

Before spiritually awakening, we feel that everything is mind. The mind, then, controlled us....If we saw something, we thought it was real. After spiritually awakening, it's different; not only have we heard that we are the creators, we now have a different way of viewing life.

To Become

a Wisdom Master, one passes through the heart

and is <u>gone</u>,[1]

<u>gone</u>[2] to the <u>beyond</u>,[3]

and <u>beyond</u>[4] the <u>beyond</u>.[5]

The first reference to *gone* denoted detachment. We can have *anything* at all in our lives, as long as we do not cling to anything. Austerities do not bring one closer to enlightenment, because to practice austerities for the sake of gaining enlightenment would be a mind-set on attachment to a process. Attachment, then, is the cause of all suffering. Without detachment, we could not come to this place of *passing through the heart*. To experience detachment, we *experience its sensations*. Its sensations are *body* sensations. Rather than saying body 'feelings,' which gets confused with emotional feelings, we will say body *sensations*....The more familiar we become with body sensations, the more easily we can move through the heart and into the *beyond* stages. We can't move to the *beyond* stages...without *practicing*, and without *living,* the detached state. First, we have to practice. We need enough experience with this detached state so that we can get a glimmer of what comes next. To get even a glimmer, we need to have *at least* some experience with this detached state.

So here is what is needed to be done. We take a look at all the 'blocks' in our lives. If we are married, then we have a 'marriage block,' and if we are single, we have a 'single block.' What does that mean?...It's not a box of some kind, it's a *block of experiences* in our memory banks. If we have jobs, we have a block of experiences about that. Even if we're retired, we still have memory; we have responsibilities, and that's our job. Whatever role in life we have, that's our job....This exercise is transcendental. We look at all these blocks of our life and notice where emotion is involved—anger, lust greed, vanity and attachment. When such emotional pictures arise, we quickly use the transcendental mind and view those areas with spiritual eyes. We go right to the Third Eye and use our bodies to help us. For example, if we have a mental vision of a spouse or a family, we put our hand out as though it were extended over that mental image and just *feel* it, without any attachment to it. We notice those body sensations without any attachment to them. We view it differently. These are things that are a part of our lives...We are the creators, we created these lives for ourselves....Now, we view those lives from this spiritual, detached state. This is a *new way* to view these situations. We're using the transcendental movement of *looking through spirituality* at blocks of our lives. If when we look at our family situations, we feel pain or fear, instantly, we know that this is *not* the kind of experience that we want to have with our families, or with our jobs, or with any situation.

We use the transcendental movement and go up to the Third Eye, so that we're *looking out* and *reaching out* with our hand, and *viewing down* at the 'block' experiences with *detachment*. We're going to have to do it all day long, so that we can get the *feel* of 'seeing.' We're not going to be able to sustain it for long periods of time, but we *will* be able to get the *feel* of this detachment from these block situations in our lives. We will notice that as we are having body sensations, sometimes those sensations may be warm or cold, but that just points out to us the way things are existing, but we're still *detached*. We don't touch it; we stay up *above* it. We feel it in our bodies, we don't *think* about it, we don't *magnify* it with the lower feelings.

So here we are *viewing situations from above*...our bodies will give us certain sensations and feelings from doing that, and that's okay. That's what the body is supposed to do. We have a well-tuned body if it's doing that. We may not be accustomed to operating our bodies in that manner, so it may be difficult for us to feel, but we don't worry about that either. That part of the fine-tuning comes in as we develop ourselves spiritually....Don't worry about feeling anything, instead, *observe* a 'block' of life. Observe it from an *objective* stance, rather than subjectively.

Look at it. What is seen?...Overall, is it a good picture? Or is it a picture that has some difficulties to it? While observing the difficulties, *we have to remain detached*, not becoming involved with guilt or fear, which is becoming *subjective* to the experience, or attached. It is vital that we stay out of attachment. When we view someone or something that we *truly* love, we must be careful; otherwise, we will start to fear for them or yearn for them, and we fall into mind passions....We just view and love....*Love is a natural expression from that detached stance*. When we are detached, we always feel love for everything that we are looking at, even though we have made some creations from emotions. This doesn't make us unhappy, because *we* are the *creators*. Viewing them from this detached place—which is the overview—if we don't get hooked into emotions about them, viewing them without really 'touching' them, we are going to see how we can make corrections. But that's not the point of this exercise. *The point of this exercise is simply for us to be able to view our lives without attachment.* This can be difficult. We view them for the sole purpose of having the experience of seeing them *without attachment*. That's the whole purpose: to view without attachment. We must have this experience before we get into this 'moving through the heart.'

We said that *to become a Wisdom Master, one passes through the heart and is gone, gone, gone to the beyond, and beyond the beyond.* We're going to continue with this passage through the heart.

74

As the journey begins,

unforeseen forces tear at the fabric of one's life

and life force.

Moaning in fever, the Traveler shifts in spirit

in a way that causes synchronization

of multiple energies.

Thus, allowances for adjustments are made.

This is not just a matter of 'sailing through the heart.' *As the journey begins, unforeseen forces tear at the fabric of one's life and life force...*This is caused by things we've set in motion in the past, things we've held fast, and now we're trying to move beyond those. In moving beyond them, our life gets ripped apart because the way we formerly saw things is no longer valid. If we 'pass through the heart,' we're going to live by an entirely different set of rules, and our lifestyle will have very little resemblance to what it was. That doesn't mean that the people are necessarily changed, but many of them will be...because it was through *false pretenses* that we held those people in our lives. If there is any kind of *fabrication* to keep certain situations in our lives, those situations and relationships will be torn from us. Of course, *we* tear them off ourselves, but it *feels* like they're being torn from us. It feels like someone is paring our skin off our bodies, which can make us sick, because it feels like there's so much being taken from us all at once. Of course, this is why real enlightenment is so rare, as rare as finding an emerald in the sea. Everything that we once held as important can no longer exist in its present form. What remains in our lives, will reshape itself.

Only the bold and adventuresome see the face of God. Only the bold and adventuresome enter the heart of God. We realize and submit to the reshaping of our entire life. It takes a great many lifetimes to prepare to pass through the heart. Our lives have to be re-shaped; otherwise, the consciousness lacks purity....There is no *compromise*. *Life* becomes refined.

If we *truly* declare that we want to become Wisdom Master, we better know that the Transhistorical Consciousness will pick our bones clean to 'clean us up.' If we're used to a longstanding livelihood, we have *to be able* to be without it. Such 'stripping away' really can't be described before, during, or after the fact, since time 'in the moment' is unified. There is a natural happiness present, a bliss without apparent cause, so we comfortably abide here in knowledge that is *pure light*. Difficulty is reconciled by opening us to pure-light demands, until we become one with the pure light.

Somehow, in this bliss, there is one thing that we have earned: *we have passed beyond ignorance*, and we have this *sense of trust*, knowing everything is fine; everything will play out as we do our part. Of course, we already had such trust when this stage began— which is the oddest thing. We don't feel 'holy,' and yet, our every breath is sacred and uplifting to the whole. We become *very quiet inside*...because, here we are, wandering in total darkness brought about by complete light. At this stage, we can't see ahead at all, because we are beyond matter in a place where there is no sight, yet there isn't any fear involved. There is so much trust, we are past fear. When we really begin the trek through the heart, we are past fear. Our body may tremble, in absence of vibration, but we're past fear. This is the beginning...the very first part. When we pass through this, the unwanted karma from the past is eradicated. All *negative karma is burned off.* We can *feel* when we've come through it. We know because, like the end of a tunnel when the light re-appears, we can now see ahead....There are things out there *for us to do*, and we couldn't see them before...because we were completely cloaked in this darkness. Then we begin to put this *creator* part of ourselves in play, *consciously*. We feel *empowered and clean*. This is how it begins—that way, moving out of the darkness. We have to learn to take care of ourselves completely. We have to learn to be totally self-reliant. In stages beyond this one, others can assist, but not this first stage.

So know that, if we scream in our hearts that we want to be Wisdom Master, *it will begin*. But it can only begin when we're no longer ignorant and we have no fear. It cannot begin before that; we wouldn't be ready. This does not mean that, in that beginning stage, we can't see the face of fear, but we will never let fear stop us. Fear is only an illusion...*It's ugly reasons are personified* into a mental monster, an aspect of identity of the one who fears.

Remember, that there is no gradual path, but there are many lifetimes involved in waking up, or in the attainment of enlightenment, so most people look at that as 'gradual.' All we're doing through all these lifetimes is coming to that place where *we ask to be the vessel*, and then it's not gradual. In other words, if we're one foot *in front of the door*, we're still not *through* the door—even though we can see through it. It doesn't matter if we're *almost* there. There's no such thing as 'almost.' *Almost* implies distance. We're still not there. We can hold a fork in our mouth, suspended between our teeth, but we still haven't eaten. We can see the food and salivate because we're hungry, but we still can't fulfill that need until we can eat it.

Gone ...

Upon first passing through the Heart,

one touches upon the place where prayers arrive.

It is here that one realizes self as compassion.

Charity arises here and one volunteers

to suffer to relieve suffering.

This *place where prayers arise* is where the Spiritualized Consciousness is able to *participate* in a special way. We are *at one* with what has already taken place in passing this far through the heart. Here, now, the suffering of others is felt, so therefore, one suffers. Out of compassion, one now *takes on a degree of suffering for others* by being in their presence. This degree of suffering is also *part of the bliss state.*

One no longer plays by the same rules as those who live an ordinary life. Most of the rules set by society and the rules of karma are bypassed, because one lives with *diffused attention* that does not attach itself to anything. One knows how to diffuse that attention and so, therefore, one doesn't play by the same rules, but instead, lives quietly. Someone who has come this distance in consciousness is *subjected to witnessing the prayers of others.* Through compassion, we do what we can to uplift others.

This *place where prayers arrive* is a place *in consciousness,* 8th level bodhisattva. Because one can hear the people's prayers, one can see the destinies others have set for themselves, through their prayers. *Destiny results from our choices* in life. However one chooses to live, describes the type of prayer that they utter. One gains insight into the meaning of those prayers and into the meaning of the consciousness that utters those prayers, and so, one gains tremendous compassion from this.

When divine consciousness sees someone suffering, it encourages what will strengthen the other. Gentleness is involved; sometimes, there is also fierceness. Such fierceness merely provides a turning point for the person who uttered the prayer.

Some may utter a hundred or so prayers a day. Inside themselves, people pray, "Please help my child...my spouse...my friend." The prayer touches upon a Spiritual (divine consciousness) Traveler who is in this realm of prayers....Once one has passed through this divine space, one is always there, because one can then hear the thoughts and prayers of others. When a person prays and a Spiritual Traveler hears a prayer, there's a *movement in the petitioner's consciousness* that usually provides an *opening* of some kind. If the one who said the prayer is truly *sincere* and open, a *greater opening* always comes to them, and they begin to see the quality of their own prayer, and what they really need to do to have it fulfilled. This is part of the 'work' of one who passes though the heart, and it gets done on a consciousness level....one consciousness inspiring the other.

The move beyond the personality is all preparation for this moment of *passing through*. Of course, this moment is part of all the other moments that we are going to eventually reflect upon. Indeed, in such service, one is *revitalized* in one's own health because *one participates, is a spiritual vessel* and not a personality. One is an *instrument*, and as an instrument, one is kept in good shape by performing the duties one requested to have. One requested the duties simply by *declaring oneself as a vessel* that is willing to go to these ends. When, at times, you call out, "How can I take a step forward?", a 'touching in consciousness' takes place. Suddenly, you relax in your physical existence; peace comes within, and the answer comes to you.

So the *Heart Traveler is a guide and a friend.* To volunteer to be a guide and a friend of that nature, one must transcend the controls of personality. We go through those recognitions and refinements so the personality no longer dictates to us. This is where Spiritual Traveling begins. *One of the beautiful parts of having glimmers of understanding, to the aspirant, is to realize the vast depths of spirituality, not minimize spirituality as something that can spring forth from a charismatic personality,* which could not be true. A Spiritual Traveler's work is timeless and unending, spontaneously taking place within the time continuum whenever a sentient impulse is received.

Gone...

When suffering flows through,

then the concession has been made,

and the second stage

has been opened to pass through.

This second Heart Chamber stage is all-knowing.

Heaven and Earth inaudibly whisper

the archives of primordial knowledge to the Traveler

from which others can be enlightened.

This first *gone* is a very, *very* important stage whereby, through compassion, there's an opening of that Heart Chamber. *When suffering flows through* that opening of the Heart Chamber, *then the concession has been made,* and that moves us to the second stage. The second *gone,* has been opened to pass through. *The second Heart Chamber stage is all-knowing.* This is 9th level bodhisattva. *Heaven and Earth inaudibly whisper the archives of primordial knowledge to the Spiritual Traveler from which others can be enlightened....*Because we have experienced suffering with others, and we still do at this stage, we carry that with us. Once an area of consciousness is opened, it remains open. It doesn't close up again.

Then, we move to another stage and it's different...more useful in that, now, because of ever-present compassion, suddenly there is greater opening...and we now have that primordial wisdom flowing through us. Whenever our attention alights on something, then information is given to us about what we see. In that way, we become the Teacher...to assist others toward enlightenment.... While much primordial knowledge has been written down, it's not necessary for the Spiritual Traveler to *read* the primordial knowledge to *know* it, although reading can sometimes be useful, because when the Spiritual Traveler sees something, knowledge of *that* opens for them. In other words, primordial knowledge doesn't open until the Spiritual Traveler's attention is drawn to something. The Spiritual Traveler is not just sitting in a flood of knowledge and hearing whisperings that are not pertinent to the moment. When we are living the moment, everywhere that our attention lights, knowledge comes as it is needed.

Moving *beyond the heart* has continual openings. Even though the Spiritual Traveler has come to the end of a text, *the openings continue*, and what has opened pours forth. The language to express this is clumsy because we're passing through all these stages, and when we say 'passing through' that usually means we're leaving something behind, but we're *not* leaving behind anything....The only thing left behind is the *ordinary* consciousness...and once one has passed the irreversible way, they only explore the *divine consciousness*. Ordinary life, then, becomes an expression of divinity. Time and space are seen as figures of physical-world speech, and instead, *NOW* is the only time form expressed. While not *of it*, the Spiritual Traveler still lives *in* the world to participate, and whatever situation is chosen to engage in, they have the primordial knowledge that opens for them as they need it.

Gone to the beyond ...

Beyond the bounds; clear of 'farther,'

cryptic silence pervades all space.

Everywhere the attention goes

unrestricted energies flow.

Here, miraculous apparitions arise without effort,

and thus ignite unconstrained and unequivocal love.

Clear of 'farther' means that one can't even describe to another *where* they are since, here, there is no 'place' and nothing to see. What exists, doesn't exist, and this sensation is both natural and supernatural. Sound echoes vibration in its purest form, and one becomes light, a transparent vessel for light to illuminate others. *Cryptic silence*, secret silence, pervades all space.

The silence is *filled with intelligence, but an intelligence beyond physical realms.* At this point in the *Heart Sutra, beyond 'farther,'* we are beyond both physical and all astral realms where tangibles abide. Yet the silence is *filled* with information about *emptiness* and the nature of silence. The nature of silence is revealed only in silence, and it is this profound silence that heals our bodies, and that balances the physical world. Such silence refills the coffers of morality, and it's a silence that *lures* one deeper and deeper, forever.

This is a place of *non-movement traveling, farther than farther.* In this place of non-movement travel, one is nourished, and one has the ability *to* nourish, meaning the nourishment received *turns one into a pedestal that holds all things up.* This stage turns the Spiritual Traveler <u>*into*</u> a pedestal that holds all things up....One is not *on* a pedestal. One <u>*is*</u> the pedestal.

The silence is *secret* because, unless one *abides* in this place, one cannot truly hear it. One is actually traveling *through* such silence, but the *silence*, being *beyond time and space*, means that one is not *experiencing* any 'movement.' One is not having *non*-movement either, because non-movement would denote that there also has to be movement. If we say it's non-movement, then there has to be an opposite, and it's *not* an opposite. *We've long passed the stage of opposites here.* One is just traversing into the silence. One is *traversing the silence.* One is *beyond openness*, because openness is a state of *allowing*. This is just silence....It cannot be compared with the silence we now recognize, except in an *as above, so below* type of thing. The nature of it, as far as consciousness is concerned, is that the Consciousness is a pedestal.

So the *glimmer* tells us that we're not only receiving gifts of primordial knowledge, but we're receiving *the ability to give* in an even grander way; or in conjunction with that pedestal Consciousness, we uplift *life*. Not the 'world,' because the world is limited to one planet. We become an interplanetary pedestal!

Beyond the beyond...

Wordless and unspeakable, incommunicable and

inconceivable; unimaginable and unbelievable

is the unutterable realm,

a place so 'real' that it is non-existent,

beyond memory and echo.

Rapture prolongs ecstasy.

Sustained rapture opens to para-nirvana, whereas

intermittent rapture returns to earth.

In the *unutterable realm, a place so 'real' that it is non-existent*...it is like something can be so light that it seems dark, so cold that it seems hot,...*so 'real' that it is non-existent,*...because it is *beyond* existence, beyond the worlds of matter. It's so real; *it is reality.* It is reality, therefore,...reality can't 'exist,' except within existence as the perpetuation of matter.

Rapture is that oneness, *that unity between purpose and heart.* It is the *coming together* between the heart and its purpose. When there is sustained rapture, rapture that intensifies to the point that there is nothing else, the Spiritualized Consciousness ceases to outflow and enters *para-nirvana.* If instead, outflowing becomes intermittent, then the Spiritual Traveler returns to earth, or remains alive on the earth plane. So, if a Spiritual Traveler maintains a physical body, then their rapture maintains an earth-connection. In intermittent rapture, when one is not in rapture, one is engaged in earthly service.

At the intermittent stage, the Spiritual Traveler can't remain in rapture for *extended* periods of time because they have a mission. So a Wisdom Master does not stay in rapture for an extended period because there is a mission. Instead, such a one accesses it momentarily, intermittently...for nectar...for refueling.

If you want to travel these realms,

listen to and contemplate the great mysterious mantra:

Gate, gate paragate, parasamgate, bodhi, svaha!

which translates:

Gone, gone, gone to beyond, and beyond the beyond,

O prajna paramita!

Rejoice!

The *Maha Prajna Paramita* that is written about in *The Wish-Fulfilling Gem Mantra* is the same *Heart Sutra* that we have just been studying. If one wants to know the true meaning of this *Gone, gone, gone beyond, O prajna paramita*...study this entire text. Contemplate this text over, and over, and over again.

Every time it is studied, it opens the student further, meaning the text initiates the student. An initiation is like driving a wedge into a block of wood, and then tapping the wedge until the wood begins to split open. The split will widen as the text is studied. Thus, the experience with the *Heart* has begun.

The initiation foundation has been established

for you to take steps that will align you

for passage through the heart.

But first you must live in a detached way.

Rejoice in THIS.

The Heart Sutra
Glossary

(Note: The definitions in this Glossary are the language and usage of HÜMÜH. They should not be construed as the single, or even the most commonly used, meaning of a specific term.)

Apparition – Any form perceivable in the physical or astral realms. All apparitions of sentient form are divinity wearing a karmic body.

Astral Body – (Mind-Vision Body) An aspect of the transcendental body (See Three Transcendental Bodies); light body without solid manifestation that is a container of all a being's individualized karma.

Astral Plane – The plane of duality where all things and all feelings exist in karmic memory.

Attachment – The fifth and most deadly of the mind passions, because it acts like glue to cement all other mind passions in place— i.e., one becomes attached to a way of being, as well as objects and people; possessiveness, or feeling that one cannot be without persons, places, situations, or things.

Attention – A focus of one's energy.

Attitude – A strong feeling that formulates a way of seeing things. Beyond an opinion; one has actually made a viewpoint out of the opinion.

Awareness – Perspective without reasoning or analytical thought. Consistently conscious of one's thought, action, and feeling. A state of pure logic.

(the) Beyond – The infinite realm of non-dual, ever-expanding divine light that is untainted by the limitations and mind-passions of *samsara*. It is characterized by wisdom and unconditional love and compassion.

Bodhisattva – A person who aspires to enlightenment through living a life of service; also, one who has attained Buddhahood who continues to live the bodhisattva life until time to enter nirvana or the state of no more karma.

Bodhisattva Levels – 1st level Bodhisattva – *The Very Joyous*; 2nd level Bodhisattva – *The Stainless*; 3rd level Bodhisattva – *The Luminous*; 4th level Bodhisattva – *The Radiant*; 5th level Bodhisattva – *The Unconquerable*; 6th level Bodhisattva – *The Manifest*; 7th level Bodhisattva – *The Distant Traveler* (the irreversible way); 8th level Bodhisattva – *The Immovable*; 9th level Bodhisattva – *The Good Intelligence*; 10th level Bodhisattva – *The Cloud of The Primordial Essence Rains upon The Summit* (perfect enlightenment). (For additional information on the various Bodhisattva levels, request information on HÜMÜH Bodhisattva Training to Enlightenment at office@humuh.org.)

Bodhisattva Vow – The HÜMÜH Bodhisattva Vow is as follows— In the presence of Wisdom Master Maticintin: *I offer my existence to the pursuit and attainment of enlightenment for myself and all other sentient beings, to live in service for the upliftment of all sentient life in a manner defined in the precepts and awarenesses set down in The Invocation For A Happy Life, NOW and FOREVER-MORE.*

Buddha – The fully enlightened consciousness; or one who has surpassed Bodhisattva Level 10.

Buddha Consciousness – (See Transhistorical Consciousness.)

Buddha-Field – A physical or astral realm which is created and maintained by an enlightened consciousness for the upliftment of sentient life. Also, a state of primal existence abiding in an enlightened consciousness.

Charity – Action or non-action that arises consciously out of compassion to relieve suffering and uplift another.

Clairvoyance – Knowledge that arises spontaneously and intuitively in the moment; ability to perceive matters beyond the range of ordinary perception.

Companion Energy – Being in tune with another so that you resonate together; total acceptance of what is, without opinion or judgment.

Compassion – Caring about the welfare of another without the emotion of attachment; has nothing to do with sympathy or internalizing the pain of others through ego-identification.

Comprehension – A capacity of mind to perceive and understand; the ability to know.

Concept – An intellectual fabrication based on reasoning and not necessarily arising from personal experience of realization.

Contemplation – A lesser level of meditation where one considers a specific Teaching, or an aspect of one's life by 'looking' at it objectively, without emotion. (See Looking Out, Overview, Meditation)

Creator – One who is responsible for bringing something into being, maintaining its nature and existence, and initiating its transformation or dissolution through the application of attention.

De-evolution – Temporary regression in spiritual evolution due to sustained self-indulgence in the mind passions, usually with great disregard for the well-being of other sentient life; this occurs until the understanding necessary for progressing toward awakening has been gained.

Deity – The creative power of knowledge manifested into a useable form. The form itself, whether it be organic (sentient) or inorganic (statue, etc.), is merely an icon of reflective proportions; that is, the form pertinent to its intention; or, in the case of a human body, the karma. A human body that reflects a deity contains a quality that is venerated by others. The venerated quality is revered because it reflects the innate nature of all human beings.

Delusion – Entrapment in an aberrant belief in some dual aspect of the illusionary world, through failure to recognize its impermanent nature; acting with habitual ignorance of the fact that spiritual development is the only thing that is real and can be transferred with us from one life to the next.

Desire – The ego-based craving for something, regardless of its consequences, which arises from the lower self and which can never be adequately fulfilled because it is reaching for something outside of oneself.

Detachment – A state of non-clinging; to relate from divinity within oneself cleanly and without the mind passions of anger, lust, greed, vanity, and attachment; the state of one in the overview or Third Eye Vision. Detachment puts us in a state of grace, which makes it possible for us to work with the flow of our dreamtime in such a manner that we live as expressions of love and compassion.

Dharma – The Primordial Teachings that are alive in all religions, although the word particularly refers to Buddhism. The primordial truth that expresses itself as the natural law which runs through all things. (See Logic.)

Direct Perception – Intuitive recognition. (See Intuition.)

Divine Consciousness – Pure consciousness or consciousness that is free from all mind passions, and is, therefore, without fear. The second of the Three Realities. (See Three Realities.)

Divinity – The prime mover or essence of reality; the divine spark that animates karma to life; the intrinsic giver, creator, and protector of life within each form.

Dream – A succession of images passing through one's mind; thus, all life is a dream and exists in all sentient life.

Duality – The realm of opposites or paradoxical existences that is part of physical life on earth, such as: plus versus minus; hot versus cold; light versus dark, etc. The real world, which co-exists with the physical, is non-dual; whereas, duality is changeable, non-duality is not changeable. (See Reality.)

Ego – The sense of self; the self-interested conglomerate of notions, attitudes, opinions, and memories that one unconsciously identifies with and which distorts and inhibits the clarity of divinity within oneself.

Entity – A being, especially one having separate, self-contained existence.

Emotion - Mind passion/poison, or various forms of anger, lust, vanity, greed, and attachment. Emotions are powerful, negative imprints of karma that form chaos and the delusion of entrapment and limitation. This happens through the ego's identifying with the emotion.

Empty – Without form, or thought, or feeling.

Energy – Spirit, life-force; that which produces the movement of electrons, atoms, and molecules, which, when they mass, form matter.

Excuse – An ego-generated, confused feeling, based on a reason not to act in alignment with the logic of the divine light within us; a fabrication of personality.

Existence –To have actual being, as opposed to appearance; the state that is common to physical objects, living beings, objects of thought and anything else; the opposite of non-existence.

Evolution – Movement toward greater spiritual awakening and the service of the whole that is a natural part of the expanding realization of the Oneness.

Fabrication – An idea, feeling, memory, object or anything that is manufactured, assembled from separate pieces, faked or forged.

Feeling – A sensation of the senses experienced in the present moment, or in the present moment relative to past events.

Form – A container of energy.

Gradual Way – The self-centered, intellectual accumulation of spiritual knowledge that does not demand living what one knows, and therefore, while it may lead to refinement of character, it cannot lead to enlightenment due to the withholding of full commitment; a preparatory stage of virtuous karma.

"Gone" – To completely pass through delusion into enlightenment by penetrating the illusions of phenomena through stages of realizing the emptiness of all form, and thereby coming into Oneness with both existence and non-existence.

Great Ocean – The Void; Divinity Itself, without personality, of which we are a part.

Happiness – The spiritual joy and contentment that arises from consciously living what we want instead of what we do not want.

Heart – The chamber of divine awareness within a human being's consciousness.

Heart Sutra/*Mahaprajnaparamita* – A mantra that liberates the heart. This Heart Sutra is chanted as *GATE GATE PARAGATE PARASAMGATE BODHI SVAHA*. (Translation: *Gone, gone, gone beyond, and beyond the beyond, O prajna paramita! Rejoice!*)

Illusion – Physical and astral manifestations. While the world we live in and objects appear real and solid, in reality, they are mental arrangements of energy and are, therefore, impermanent. Thus, our bodies and the world we live in are impermanent, mere capabilities of the dreamtime.

Inconceivable – Beyond rational, intellectual comprehension.

Incommunicable – Beyond the ability to convey, requiring direct experience.

Initiation – An opening or opportunity for the next step in spiritual advancement granted to the student by the Wisdom Master; also, a spiritual level. (For information on the Initiations of HÜMÜH, contact office@humuh.org.)

Intrinsic Awareness – The spark of divine consciousness that is an inborn, natural part of the creative ability.

Intuition – Immediate comprehension without reasoning; a function of the intrinsic divinity within us that can relay knowledge about what is perceived when we are acting with the free will of conscious awareness; a tremendous power of the heart center.

(The) Invocation for a Happy Life – A HÜMÜH prayer that evokes the divinity within oneself by teaching one about the tenets of a happy life.

Karma – Cause and effect; also the compounded, complete results of thoughts, words, and actions as they have affected one or more sentient beings; a natural result of an action; a reaction to the stillness; the result of the movement of a cycle.

Life-Force – Vitality, flow of energy from divinity that animates to life.

Logic – The divine overview, which is a combination of the dual elements, leaving it free to perceive from the third element: the whole, or unity of a thing or situation; the dharma truth which is the simple, mutable, dynamic law of the way energy works and flows through the movements and manifestations of all that exists, whether we are aware of it or not.

Looking In – To put attention on one's feelings and mull them over; to internalize emotions, situations, and events and make the focus be about ego instead of the good of the whole.

Looking Out – To unselfconsciously put mindful attention on something for the good of the whole; to see all aspects of a situation from the overview.

Mahaprajnaparamita – (See Heart Sutra.)

Maticintin – Means *Virtuous Giver*; name of the founder and spiritual leader of HÜMÜH Buddhism. A name assigned by Sakyamuni Buddha and later revealed by Padmasambhava to Dorji Dudjom at the Tiger's Nest Monastery in Bhutan. This monastery was later destroyed by fire when the Chinese challenged its location on the Bhutanese/Tibetan border in 1995. Prior to that, the monks and the monastery contents were moved to safety. Also, Wisdom Master Maticintin's name at birth.

Meditation – State of relaxed, quiet mind, where mind-chatter ceases and everything disappears except light; bliss state of emptiness in which knowingness can arise; extended awareness; Third Eye Vision; in its lesser levels, contemplation. (See Quiet Mind.)

Memory – All that is familiar from all lifetimes lived.

Mental States – Habitual ways of thinking; ideas, notions, and attitudes adopted from others—all illusionary.

Mind – The mental screen where all images are projected. The quality of images projected reveal one's state of consciousness. Mind is not an entity in itself. (See also Universal Mind.)

Mindfulness – A state of mental vigilance whereby one practices, and later maintains, consistent awareness of one's every thought, word, feeling, and action. A state of being aware that one is aware. Also, Third Eye Vision, or extended awareness.

Mind Chatter – Internal conversations; originates from a mental state of uncertainty.

Mind Passions/Poisons – Anger, lust, greed, vanity, and attachment and all the subtle, related infractions such as disappointment and jealousy, all of which arise from fear. (See Chart pg. 36). Mind passions distort perception and bring unwanted sensations, unfavorable conditions, and ill fortune.

Mulling – Obsessive, repetitive thinking.

Myth – The unconscious fabrication of one's life. (See Fabrication.)

Negative Karma – Karma that creates unfavorable conditions.

Notion – An idea of what we think something is, or of how to get something, usually accompanied with emotion and based on past experience, applied without openness to the present moment.

Now – Awareness that time and space are illusions and that time is not linear: past, present, and future are simultaneously and actively linked in the present moment; therefore, what happens in the present moment is always affecting both the past and the future.

Oblivion – Loss of awareness of the light of our divinity through the pursuit of habitual ego-behavior. This results in forgetting that we are the responsible creators of our lives and that our circumstances cannot get worse, change, or improve, except through our direction.

Obsession – An addictive, compulsive drive to act in a certain habitual way; a fixated expression that arises from lust. An obsession destroys life by blocking the wisdom of divinity.

Openness – To be without limitations of unconscious attitudes or opinions; a complete vulnerability to what we want, a stance of willingness to let go of the habitual and allow the unknown of what we truly want to change us.

Paramita – Another shore; the attainment of transcending a lower level of consciousness to a higher one; relates to the transcendental mind; also, the verbal 'formula' to guide a spiritual student in the recognitions necessary to come to a particular realization.

Perception – Power of apprehension; the result of observation; an awareness of the elements of the environment or what is being looked at; when arising from spiritual awareness, the direct knowledge of the essence of a thing and how it came to be.

Personality – The unreal particular manner or style through which karma expresses itself that cloaks divinity in an individual. If unconscious, synonymous with the limitations of the emanations of ego's disposition; if utilized with conscious, spiritual awareness, a divine tool.

Phenomena – The manifestations within the physical and astral worlds where life's objects, relationships, and circumstances are dreamed in reflection of one's karma.

Physical Body – A manifestation of individualized karma.

Positive Karma – Karma that creates favorable conditions.

Post-Meditation – Maintaining the meditative state of awareness outside of formal times of sitting meditation so that it becomes the way one lives daily life. (See Meditation and Quiet Mind.)

Prajna – To have a conscious awareness of the consciousness of wisdom.

Prajna Paramita – The *paramita* of consciousness which transcends into liberation.

Prayer – An evocation of the divine energies, which can only be used successfully when petitioning unconditional assistance; also, the conscious and unconscious pleas of those still caught in the suffering of *samsara* that are heard by the Spiritual Traveler at a certain stage of realization.

Primordial – Beginingless time; first.

Purity – A state of primordial naturalness untainted by self-interest; a state untarnished by identity, except that it exists in equanimity.

Quiet Mind – Listening to the silence in a relaxed state of consciousness, uninterrupted by mind chatter; maintaining inner silence without will power or mind control.

Rapture – The bliss that results when heart and purpose connect; ecstasy.

Realization – A state of conscious, focused attention that fuses one with the object of one's attention, i.e., becoming one with The Teachings of the Path of Divine Consciousness; once something is truly realized, it is then fully embraced and consciously lived.

Responsibility – A spiritual stance that accepts that one is the creator of all the circumstances of one's life and, therefore, karmically accountable for how one's words, thoughts, feelings, and actions affect the good of the whole; a stance of empowered freedom.

Resonance – Responding to the One with what is; companion energy.

Samsara – A succession of rebirths that a person goes through within the various modes of existence. The cause of *samsara* is desire or craving, and delusion. The lives of the unenlightened are referred to as *samsara*.

Self – The expression of being that reflects one's myth, ego, and/or personality; same as 'little self.'

Self-Discipline – A state of ecstatic being whereby one spiritually practices for the joy that is attained.

Sentient – A category that includes humans, animals, reptiles, birds, insects, and fish. All sentient beings have consciousness, even though their levels of consciousness differ.

Silence – An inner space of openness and equanimity that is within the Void, whereby one can perceive events and energy within the environment without thought. Also, a place where Oneness is realized, and related powers develop; realm of spiritual Light.

Skycliffe – HÜMÜH Monastery and Retreat Centre in Westbridge, B.C.

Space – The unmanifested energy between forms.

Spirit – The energy of the Divine Consciousness, the Void.

Spiritual Student – One who seriously commits to follow the guidance of a Wisdom Master, and not only studies the Teachings, but takes responsibility to develop the self-discipline necessary to live their life *through* the Teachings, rather than simply make the Teachings an interesting part of their life.

Spiritual Traveler – (See Traveler.)

Suffering – Distress caused by living illogically; anguish from persisting in a condition that is not wanted instead of choosing what brings about what is wanted; the result of a conflict within oneself from trying to go in two directions at once.

Sutra – Sanskrit for *"thread;"* refers to discourses by the Buddha.

Synchronization – To unite multiple energies in a harmony of purposeful timing.

Three Realities – 1) The Void or God; 2) Divine consciousness, which realizes the Void, and 3) Life, also called the dreamtime.

Three Transcendental Bodies – 1) Body in which a bodhisattva attains enjoyment in the Samadhis; 2) body assumed by those who are completely enlightened, according to the class of beings being sustained; 3) the body in which those who are completely enlightened receive their intuition of Dharmakaya.

Transhistorical Consciousness – The One Consciousness that exists, has always existed, and will always exist in all spiritual adepts throughout eternity.

Traveler – Same as Spiritual Traveler; one who consciously journeys through physical lifetimes with a commitment to awaken, seeking enlightenment for the sake of all sentient life; one who, at some point, dedicates their spiritual journey to becoming a Wisdom Master in order to guide others in seeking enlightenment; also, a Wisdom Master who endlessly explores the infinite realms of spiritual awareness as an act of compassion for the whole.

Unimaginable – Beyond the forms and images in the memory bank of ordinary consciousness.

Universal Mind – The One Mind that reflects everything and nothingness. This 'One Mind' is engulfed by the three existences: the past, present, and future, and all its mental images.

Viewpoint – An attitude or angle through which one perceives the object of their attention.

Wisdom – The knowingness that dictates right thought, speech, and action. Complete wisdom manifests in one's life and circumstances through pure attention.

Wisdom Master – One who has passed beyond bodhisattva level 10 and gained entrance into the *Unspeakable Realm;* a Spiritual Teacher who has reached this level or beyond. An enlightened Spiritual Master/Teacher possesses inherent knowledge (rather than learned knowledge); that is, He or She literally knows everything of the natural world and how inventions arise from that. He or She knows how the universe is formed—past, present, future, and how the karma of all life forms are intertwined within it. Moreover, such a Master is God-Realized and has conscious access to the Void. Such a Master in this present life is one who attained enlightenment in a previous life, which is why the knowledge they possess now is inherent (realized), rather than newly acquired.

(The) Wish-Fulfilling Gem Mantra – Called the mantra for the cultivation of the enlightened mind. A 66-stanza sacred mantra, mostly in Sanskrit, that is available to students, in the written form, at the discretion of the Wisdom Master. To receive this mantra, the student agrees to protect it from desecration and not to share it with anyone.

www.HUMUH.org

√ *Check Here*

I would like to receive information about other books by Wisdom Master Maticintin.
I would like to receive information about becoming a student of HÜMÜH.
I would like to be added to your mailing list and receive information about events
with Wisdom Master Maticintin.
I would like to receive *free* the Daily Wisdom Teaching by e-mail.

Please Print Clearly or Call: 1(800) 336-6015

Name: _____

Address: _____

City & State/Province: _____

Zip/Postal Code: _____ Country: _____

E-Mail: _____

- -

√ *Check Here*

I would like to receive information about other books by Wisdom Master Maticintin.
I would like to receive information about becoming a student of HÜMÜH.
I would like to be added to your mailing list and receive information about events
with Wisdom Master Maticintin.
I would like to receive *free* the Daily Wisdom Teaching by e-mail.

Please Print Clearly or Call: 1(800) 336-6015

Name: _____

Address: _____

City & State/Province: _____

Zip/Postal Code: _____ Country: _____

E-Mail: _____

HÜMÜH™
Transcendental Buddhism™
Transcendental Awareness Institute
P.O. Box 2700
Oroville, WA 98844
USA

HÜMÜH™
Transcendental Buddhism™
Transcendental Awareness Institute
P.O. Box 701
Osoyoos, BC V0H 1V0
Canada